A STEP-BY-STEP GUIDE TO

WRITING APPLICATIONS and ESSAYS

I'M APPLYING TO COLLEGE: NOW WHAT? A STEP-BY-STEP GUIDE TO WRITING APPLICATIONS AND ESSAYS

1405 SW 6th Avenue • Ocala, Florida 34471 • Phone 352-622-1825 • Fax 352-622-1875
Website: www.atlantic-pub.com • Email: sales@atlantic-pub.com
SAN Number: 268-1250

Library of Congress Cataloging-in-Publication Data

Names: Erikson, Angela.
Title: I'm applying to college, now what? : a step-by-step guide to writing applications & essays to make your work stand out / by Angela Erikson.
Description: Ocala, Florida : Atlantic Publishing Group, Inc., 2018. | Includes bibliographical references and index.
Identifiers: LCCN 2017057160 (print) | LCCN 2017060663 (ebook) | ISBN 9781620231968 () | ISBN 9781620231951 (pbk. : alk. paper) | ISBN 9781620232460 (library edition : alk. paper) | ISBN 1620231956 (alk. paper)
Subjects: LCSH: College applications—Handbooks, manuals, etc. | Universities and colleges—Admission—Handbooks, manuals, etc. | Essay—Authorship—Problems, exercises, etc. | College student orientation—United States—Handbooks, manuals, etc.
Classification: LCC LB2351.5 (ebook) | LCC LB2351.5 .E75 2018 (print) | DDC 378.1/616—dc23
LC record available at https://lccn.loc.gov/2017057160

Printed in the United States

INTERIOR LAYOUT AND JACKET DESIGN: Nicole Sturk

Over the years, we have adopted a number of dogs from rescues and shelters. First there was Bear and after he passed, Ginger and Scout. Now, we have Kira, another rescue. They have brought immense joy and love not just into our lives, but into the lives of all who met them.

We want you to know a portion of the profits of this book will be donated in Bear, Ginger and Scout's memory to local animal shelters, parks, conservation organizations, and other individuals and nonprofit organizations in need of assistance.

– Douglas & Sherri Brown,
President & Vice-President of Atlantic Publishing

Contents

INTRODUCTION

For many students, the thought of going to college is a stressful, nail-biting prospect. Students may ask themselves things like "What am I doing? How can I accomplish this? How am I going to get in? Where will I go? What will I do once I get there?" It's often difficult to find easy answers to these questions, mainly because there are none ("easy," that is). But nothing worthwhile in life ever comes easily; the decision to attend college will be one of the more invaluable because it reaps a harvest that will last a lifetime.

With any luck, you and your parents have been communicating about this decision, and they have been supportive and yet respectful of your need to think for yourself, but the college dilemma can be made even worse by continual questions from well-meaning relatives, teachers, and friends — especially those who frame their questions with a definite bias:

"You know, Ohio State football has some of the best tailgate parties."

"I know a few of the alumni at UCLA who are faculty members; you know — I am sure they would recommend you."

"So, are you going to Iowa? I know my older sister truly enjoyed their Fine Arts program; did you know she got her Master of Fine Arts degree (MFA) just last year?"

"I am a cinch to get into wherever I apply; if you came with me, we could get an off-campus apartment."

"I wish you were coming with me to Hollins — I'm really going to miss you."

"We do hope you will stay right here in (insert your hometown here) for your studies, dear — how will we ever get along without you? And who will help us with the yard, and eat our pies and cookies?"

We know you want to make the most of the educational opportunity — that is the most important reason for going to college. This doesn't mean you can't enjoy Uncle Joe's tailgate parties; however, they shouldn't be the final determining factor in whether Ohio State would be right — or wrong — for you. Buckeye tailgate parties are optional, you can choose to go or steer clear; the thing to consider first and foremost is whether Ohio State offers the program you want. If you're looking forward to those parties as an occasional means of recreation and socializing in between studying for a professional and rewarding career, this indicates a healthy balance and is no indication that you won't be successful. Uncle Joe would probably agree!

While educational goals should be your first concern, there are many factors to weigh when choosing and applying to colleges. You'll also need to consider cost, location, academic expectations, extracurricular opportunities, social and networking opportunities, and realistic chance you will be accepted. Because an overview is always advisable, we'll briefly explore these questions in the first five chapters of the book.

Beginning with Chapter 6, we're diving right into what for many is the most "frightening" aspect of college application: the application essay. Please notice the quotation marks around that adjective. The application essay is nothing to fear — at least, no more than any other challenge you will face along the way. And hear this, right here and now: college will require writing. **A lot of it.**

But wait — don't stress! You will most likely end up doing just fine. Writing is like anything else; even if it scares you now, with a little practice, you will soon find it easier. Chapters 7 through 9 more thoroughly discuss what the admissions committees look for, and Chapter 10 is devoted to brainstorming ideas. Chapters 11-13 share some tips for writing, and especially how writing applies to this essay. Chapter 14 summarizes many of the key points covered in the first 13 chapters, and also adds some different tips and perspectives.

In the Appendix, you will find a starter list of scholarship websites. Please bear in mind that even if the site is talking about, for example, "Spring 2016," chances are that this is a repeating scholarship offer and it will be beneficial for you to look into the listing more closely.

There is also a Bibliography that includes further resources about college admissions and application essays. Most of these books can either be checked out from your local library or purchased online. There is no one right book to read; each one can contribute valuable advice to your overall college-application strategy.

A final few words of introduction: in this book, we have attempted to not give you the official, formal *how-to's* of the full college application process; as the Bibliography will attest, there are many books and articles on that subject. What we hope to do here is offer a more practical, down-to-earth look at the challenges you will face — especially when it comes to the writing — and how best to address them.

CHAPTER 1

Are You Cut Out For College?

Do you remember eighth grade? By the time you are reading this book, you're probably well past that period, but this turning point of your school life is where it all began: the college admissions preparation process.

You might not have even realized it at the time, but it all started that day that you chose your ninth-grade classes. You probably already knew what subjects you liked and were good at, such as science, math, art, or English. From then on, every class was an experience that led you along the journey to your graduation — and to whatever may appear next on the horizon.

But what exactly is next?

The following question may appear simple on the surface, but it leads to many others more difficult to answer: *Are you cut out for college?* The key to answering this question takes a bit of self-reflection. Ask yourself the following questions:

- Who am I? Where do I come from? What is my background?

- What are my talents? What are my strengths? What are my weaknesses?

- Do I like school? Do I put forth my best effort in school?

- What kinds of extracurricular activities do I enjoy?

- Will my skills be best put to use in college?

These important initial questions must be asked (and there are many others to come) when addressing the issue of college and considering how to proceed with the college application process.

You might need a lot of time to think this through. The most important thing to remember is that you must use this personal reflection as a means to make the decision on your own whether or not to attend college. This decision should not be dictated by somebody else, and it should not be based on where your friends decide to attend college, or what school(s) your parents, relatives, or siblings attended. This decision should be purely personal, and it should reveal who you are as a person and the type of growth that you would like to achieve.

You must also be honest with yourself (hey, you will know upfront if you are lying, and everybody else will soon find out) and willing to admit that there are areas in which you would be fooling yourself — and therefore cheating yourself — if you were to be anything other than truthful.

Identifying your personal strengths and weaknesses might be difficult. After being told all your life not to brag, you may hesitate to "toot your own horn" by calling attention to your most dominant strengths (such as *I am in the top 5 percent of my class* or *I am the varsity quarterback*). However, naming and building upon these strengths is important to determine the way you will expand your potential from this point forward. If you indeed are near the top of your class or have strong athletic abilities, this is not bragging; it is fact. Of course, there is a way to go about it and a way not to go about it: *I have been the varsity quarterback since my sophomore year, and after a ton of hard work and close games, our team took the Division title last year as* opposed to *I beat everyone out in my sophomore year and have thrown more game-winning passes than Coach said anybody else at my school ever has.*

On the other hand, you might be hesitant to admit to what you perceive — or rightfully know — to be your weaknesses. Most people learn over the course of time that weaknesses and strengths oftentimes offset each other. In fact, strengths and weaknesses don't necessarily have to stand alone and apart from each other; there can be a co-mingling of the two. For example, you might recognize that you are skilled at science — based on your grades — but you are also interested in creative alternatives you find more interesting.

Bear in mind that your education plans will go more smoothly if you play to your strengths. Also remember that your choices are not always limited to either/or. You can apply to colleges and universities that will best accommodate your creative talents along with offering a top-notch education in science.

After reflecting, you may want to examine how your personal strengths and weaknesses will be used in the college environment and if your expectations are realistic. If these expectations are too grand (for example, attending Harvard University with a 2.5 GPA), you may need to readjust them. This is by no means a failure in your efforts or in the planning process. Let's be real: some of us shine brighter in different areas than others. You must examine what types of gifts you have, and what those gifts, or skills, can bring to the collegiate table.

Under license from Shutterstock.com

For some students, Ivy League is the only sensible option; for others, a vocational or technical school will best suit their needs. The thing to realize is that as far as society is concerned, the skills learned in all ranges of educational institutions are equally important; yet, as far as you are concerned, the "importance" of your area of study and own priorities are an individual question.

The following beginning of a Case Study is a good example:

CASE STUDY:

AN UNCERTAIN STUDENT'S DILEMMA

After a sub-par performance in high school, I was really worried about going to college but knew that I had to do it — and, in spite of being worried, I really wanted to do it. After thinking about it for six months, I sent applications to Wright State University (Dayton, OH), the University of Cincinnati, and the College of Mount St. Joseph, a private institution on Cincinnati's west side.

I selected these schools because of their proximity to my residence. More specifically, I chose to apply to Mt. St. Joseph because of the scholarship they offered me to play on their soccer team. But when I weighed everything, "the Mount" is a little hard to get to from where I live and their academic expectations would be fairly high. The University of Cincinnati is easily accessible from home, but almost "too close," and the area's pretty congested, so my final choice was Wright State because it gave me enough distance to be independent and start a new life while still being close enough to family and friends.

— Pam Lasko, Student, Wright State University

It should go without saying that attending college should be your choice, just as your choice of which college to attend. Nevertheless, your parents should play a part in helping you make your decision. You probably can already see that there could be some differences between your desires and theirs. The key here is to include them, even in small ways, as you begin your reflection.

Plus, somewhere along the way, give some thought to these two additional questions:

- Are there any familial expectations of me in regards to college? Can I satisfy, or do I truly want or need to satisfy, those expectations?

- Do I want to go to college, or is that just something that my family wants me to do?

As in the original questions at the beginning of this chapter, there is no one but yourself who can answer those questions. "Following in Daddy's footsteps" might appeal to some students, and it may be what you truly want to do, but if the shoes do not fit and your educational-desire "feet" are of a different size, you are likely to end up tripping if you try to force yourself to follow his path.

Similarly, if the only reason you intend to go to college is because you have been convinced/coerced/forced by well-intentioned parents and relatives to do so, you are not likely to do well. You may end up failing or even dropping out. But once again, the key to avoiding disharmony is to communicate, communicate, communicate.

For the purposes of this book, we're going forward with the assumption that you do want to go to college for your own reasons, and are openly inviting your parents to join in the conversation.

Now, college decisions are not generally the types that are made in a single sit-down parent-child pow-wow. By sharing the self-reflection process with your parents, you are inviting their trust by showing your own. Sharing doesn't mean revealing every deep-down innermost secret to your folks, but assuring them that you are giving serious thought before making any big decisions. If they know you are making a conscientious choice, they are much more likely to be open to your decisions — whatever they may be.

Finally, once you make a decision, don't be afraid to get help whenever necessary to help you through the application process. Although personal reflection will help you make wise decisions about college, don't do this based only on your own opinion. Ask for advice from people who have experienced life longer than you, such as parents, teachers, guidance counselors, older siblings, or friends. You are much more likely to achieve your college goals when you understand and accept the challenges you're up against and are backed by the support and encouragement of your loved ones and friends.

The following case study is a good example of how combining personal choice and the advice of others helped one student (and, introduces the concept of writing an application essay which will be discussed at length in Chapter 8):

CASE STUDY:

ENOUGH SUPPORT TO MAKE MY OWN COLLEGE DECISION

As a senior in high school facing the college application process, I was required to write a personal statement (letter of intent) to be included with the application paperwork. At the age of 17, considering my goals and future intentions was a fairly overwhelming concern. To avoid nervousness, I first approached this statement with the hope of appearing mature and goal-oriented, and not just a teenager looking to party in college.

When starting this statement, I first looked for the support and advice of my parents. Having influenced me to be responsible and build my future goals, my parents were probably the best help I could have hoped for. With their advice, I began my statement with a very brief biographical introduction. The university would get everything they needed from my transcripts and test scores and did not need to know my life story. I then figured it would be most important to express my intent to take my education seriously and what goals I hoped to accomplish through the acquisition of a degree.

So, after my brief introduction I pointed my statement directly into my intended major, which was Biology. I then directed my statement to the goals I hoped to achieve from this major and my hope to attend medical school upon graduation. I believed that in focusing on my future goals and the intentions I held for my college education, the university would see me as a student, rather than simply an applicant.

Again, I must say that I had my parents to thank for helping me focus on the future and what I wanted to get out of my education, and I recommend that anyone writing a letter of intent or personal statement of this kind request the advice of a parent or other adult whom you respect and trust.

— Sara McIntosh, Quality Assurance Editor, Convergys

To wrap up this chapter, remember that a period of self-reflection and an honest assessment of who you are and where you want to go in life are vital to your college aspirations. Look over your life's history, recognize your strengths, and admit your weaknesses. These factors have made you who you are today, and they also demonstrate how prepared you are for the college experience. Your personality and some of the choices you have already made in your young life may have prepared you quite well for this next experience, while others may have led you astray.

Where you are emotionally, scholastically, socially, and physically at this stage will play an important role in how you conduct your life from this point forward. If college is in your future, you should start preparing yourself sooner, rather than later, for what is to come, including the application process.

Applying to college can be daunting. However, with a well-established support system in your corner, you will find that the process may be more fun and even more exciting than you ever imagined. As a human being, you will be weak in some ways and strong in others, but with perseverance and motivation, you can be confident of success.

CHAPTER 2

What College Will Best Suit You?

Y ou may have a lot of questions at this point in time.

- Do you want to stay near your hometown or go far away to college?

- Which colleges are most appealing to you?

- Which colleges are in your price range?

- Which colleges provide scholarship opportunities?

- Which colleges have the best programs in your field of interest?

- If you are undecided on a major, which colleges provide the best all-around academic and social/extracurricular experiences for you?

If you've determined that you are indeed cut out for college, you've made an educational decision that will affect the rest of your life. For right now, though, know that for at least the next two to four years, you will be engulfed in books, papers, assignments, and other activities that will play a major role in your young adulthood.

Now you're wondering how to decide where to go for college. To answer this extremely important question, you must think back to your personal reflection in Chapter 1. This reflection will help you determine the type of academic program you wish to enter, and the overall characteristics that you consider most valuable in the college experience. Look at all options presented to you, and evaluate them based on that critical self-examination.

As it did with the *Are you cut out for college?* question, asking *Where should I go?* leads to many more questions. Remember that there is no universal order of importance. In reality, a concern you have might not have even crossed another student's mind. It's up to you to decide what matters most and how important each issue is to you. Lists are helpful; they help you see things visually and enable you to rank these criteria in the order in which they are most important to you. For example, take a look at the first question on the list above...

Do You Want To Stay Near Your Hometown Or Go Far Away To College?

Although many high school students can't wait to leave home, the fact is that some, whether because of money or family obligations, don't even consider leaving. On the other hand, if a student really wants to attend an out-of-state college because it meets his or her exact needs (and no local institutions offer a similar program), there may be no choice but to leave.

When looking at the go-away vs. stay-home dilemma, if one or the other is vital to your situation, well, there you are — that decision has been made. However, if both options are open, you can focus on other issues without having to check and see if your local schools offer your chosen course.

One word of advice: don't spend time on any decisions that can easily be answered or eliminated. For example, let's say your local university has the program you are looking for, it is rated incredibly high in academic circles, and you already know your parents have said they simply cannot afford to send you anywhere else; don't waste time daydreaming or fancying what "might have been." Be realistic and understand that sometimes the first door will open on to other opportunities; if you start well in your local school, who knows where you might end up?

And, even if leaving town is the option, you can still never be sure where you will end up.

CASE STUDY:

FROM START TO FINISH — A TALE OF THREE CITIES

When I was in high school, Vanderbilt University was almost within walking distance of my home. It offered great programs, but I chose an elite women's college in the South, Sophie Newcomb of Tulane University, near New Orleans, Louisiana. After a year, I transferred to a school with a more down-to-earth diverse student population, Ohio University in Athens, Ohio. There I earned a Bachelor of Arts Degree in Psychology and positioned myself to offer semi-professional therapy to my "spoon-fed," "lost," and "need-to-find-myself" peers.

During the summer following my second year at Ohio University, I found out that I could earn more credits toward my degree by taking some courses at Vanderbilt. I went home for the summer, took the courses, and then returned to Athens.

After graduating with a B.A., I discovered that my career opportunities would broaden with an advanced degree, so I again headed south to Tulane University and earned a Master's Degree in Social Work. My first "real job" after graduation was Instructor in Clinical Social Work with the Medical School at the University of Cincinnati.

— Joan S. Lasko, M.S.W.

So, as you can see, the plan you have mapped out based on geography may lead in directions you never expect — including back home, even if only temporarily.

Remember that where you begin college may not be the same place from which you graduate; the important thing is to get your education underway, do well, and see what develops from there. Applying to a local college isn't the same as being stuck forever in your hometown.

Which Colleges Are Most Appealing To You?

The two most important words are at the end: what kind of college appeals to you?

More than just the academics: are you big on college athletics, either as a participant or fan? You almost certainly would not want to go to a small college with only a few intramural sports; you want more action on the field and/or court. On the other hand, if you are of a more studious nature and couldn't care less about sports, the continual noise and hype and sports partying that goes with a Big Ten school could set your nerves on edge.

You might consider the climate and weather. If you are a quarterback in Florida, you might not be too successful playing on the windswept University of North Dakota campus. You may have a personal preference natural perks as being close to the beach, or mountains for hiking and skiing. Do you find extreme heat or cold unbearable? Are you easily depressed by too many cloudy, rainy days?

And what about the town closest to the college? In the case study above, Ms. Lasko was happy to be so close to New Orleans and its colorful French Quarter and endless seafood bounty, but another student might leave because of all the noise and the oppressive heat, or allergies to seafood.

And while thinking about the town, you might also want to consider more practical issues, such the possibilities of part-time employment; what kind of opportunities are there for a student who wants to "earn as you learn?" Does the town offer a good, clean, and safe environment?

Or, do any of the above questions truly matter to you?

Here is a good place for you to start eliminating some options. Unless you have a good reason to consider a college that initially doesn't appeal to you, don't waste time on it.

What's a good reason to go to a college that's not your first choice? Let's say you are that Florida football player, and you are offered a full-ride scholarship to UND — you may have to seriously consider buying some heavy clothing and heading north. Realistically speaking, you are likely to spend the better part of the next several years in the college's environment, so make sure you take everything into consideration when making your decisions.

You need to look at your own preferences in determining which college or university is most attractive and appealing *to you*. You may be concerned with classroom size, teacher-to-student ratio, and other non-athletic extra-curricular activities. Are you interested in the "Greek" life (sororities and fraternities)? Are you interested in working on a school's newspaper or participating on debate teams? There are most likely other considerations unique to you, and you should seriously examine them without feeling ridiculous; their importance is yours alone to evaluate.

Which Colleges Are In Your Price Range?

Let's talk about your professional goals. You've made the decision to attend college, and now you must decide if you wish to pursue an Associate's or

Bachelor's degree. For many majors, an Associate's degree may be all that is required to find a job and begin your career within that particular job market. For other programs or majors, a Bachelor's degree or higher may be required, and therefore you should look into four-year colleges or universities that provide these degrees. Obviously, the costs will be different; yet, for the most part, the two-year Associate's programs can be applied to eventual Bachelor's work.

What about price range? With college tuition cost rising every year, this is an incredibly important question to ask. How much is tuition going to cost? What about room and board? Are these affordable? If you can't pay for them on your own, what types of loans, grants, and scholarships are available? You might have the grades to attend an Ivy League university, but your dream may not be realized without serious financial difficulty. Even many universities that offer online programs charge high tuition rates that are difficult for many students to manage.

So, exactly what costs are we talking about? Recent surveys state that the average student at a community college in the 2016-2017 school year paid around $4,914 for in-state tuition or $8,659 for out-of-state-tuition. A student at an in-state public college for the 2016-2017 academic year would pay $24,610. A student at a private college paid an average of $49,320.[1]

1. collegedata.com, 2017
   communitycollegereview.com, 2017

Under license from Shutterstock.com

For some, one good way to begin a college education may be to attend a local two-year community college that has more affordable tuition. Students can remain in the home environment to eliminate room and board rates, and most credits can transfer to four-year colleges or universities in future years. For many students, and/or more precisely their parents, the cost of a college education is alarming, and therefore these issues must be seriously considered in the earliest stages of the college admission process.

Don't let all of this money talk frighten you! With a bit of hard work on earning good grades, along with searching for scholarships and grants, you can still achieve your college goals.

Which Colleges Provide Scholarship Opportunities?

When considering colleges, think about your specific skills and talents that will help you earn a grant or scholarship to offset the costs of tuition. This also shows how important it is to keep up your grades throughout high school to improve the chances of obtaining scholarships.

The number of scholarships available to students today are too many to count. They are based upon a wide variety of criteria, including those related to cultural background, gender, extracurricular activities, financial need, and other skills and talents that students may possess. It's important to look for as many scholarship opportunities as possible.

Please note that some scholarships may apply to any institution, while others are offered for use at a specific school. High school counselors often have good leads on what scholarships are available. There is more than enough information readily available on the web, a good "beginning sampler" of which is included in Appendix I at the end of this book.

Which Colleges Have The Best Programs In Your Field Of Interest?

How do you know which colleges or universities offer a major in your field of interest? The answer is simple: research.

Again, counselors and the internet will prove to be invaluable. You must address your options through a personalized research endeavor that will enable you to single out those colleges and universities that fit your specific criteria, including those related to major or field of study. If you do not fully research your options, you may find yourself without a clear vision regarding your college education.

You must look at your options thoroughly and without hesitation to make educated choices for your future. If your major is biology, you'll want to pursue colleges with strong biology programs. If you prefer accounting, look at schools with highly competitive business courses. Even if a particular school meets all your needs so far as climate, location, extracurriculars and such, it just doesn't make sense to attend a college or university that is strong in artistic studies when you're a bio major on the premed track.

Which Colleges Provide The Best All-Around Academic And Extracurricular Experiences?

Many students enter the college application process with an undecided major. There is nothing wrong with this. Even after self-reflection, you may still be unsure where your true college-related talents or strengths lie. Don't get discouraged; remember that an "Undecided" major is not the end of the world. About half of your college classes will be what are known as "core classes" — in other words, they are required of everyone, no matter what your chosen major might be. Many students begin college by taking these core courses and then find themselves developing new interests, learning their strengths, and shaping their eventual decision on a major as they complete the required course load.

As you decide on a major, consider what else the school has to offer. Go back to the list you made (location, climate, extracurriculars and such), organizing your preferences in the order of importance; this should help you weight all the factors objectively. You have to find the balance that is best for you and find a college or university that help you grow in knowledge and experience in the best possible way.

So . . . what's next?

The moment that you begin to take the college application process seriously, start researching. You will probably find that you are more than prepared for the challenges that await you. As the ancient Chinese proverb says, *The journey of 1,000 miles begins with one step*, and that first step will always be the hardest because you know there are still so many more to go — but you also will never get anywhere without putting one foot in front of the other and getting started.

When you have made these initial selections, call or email the specific colleges to request more information and start asking your teachers, counselors, parents, and other acquaintances questions. What do they know about these colleges? What is their reputation? Has anybody you have known attended these colleges? If so, what were their experiences? Would they recommend these colleges to you? Are they a good fit? What else can they tell you about them? If you do not ask these questions, you may never get the answers that you need to make an informed decision.

Remember, of course, that your decision is your own. While getting feedback from others is helpful, bear in mind that your goals and the things you look for may not be the same as theirs.

Again, let's take Uncle Joe: his memories of Ohio State are obviously fond, but Joe's experiences may not in actuality apply to you — and also don't forget the age difference. Things today at Ohio State University may be a far cry from his memories. You have no doubt also heard the expression *One man's trash is another man's treasure*; the same is true here. Joe's fond memories may be offset by his brother Ted's intense dislike for the institution that was strong enough to result in his changing colleges in mid-stream. Ask questions, listen to the answers, but do not go strictly by what others say — either negative or positive — because even the most well-meaning of them might accidentally mislead you.

Yes, by all means ask as many people and solicit as much personal information as you can, but ultimately — again — this is your decision to make. Look online, request brochures, and keep your own agenda in mind. Review the materials you requested from various colleges as much as possible. Not only will these materials provide you with physical descriptions of the college campuses, they will also help you see if the schools align with your specific needs. A single glimpse at one of these books may be the deciding factor in choosing a college or university.

The questions raised in this chapter give a glimpse into the various criteria that should be evaluated when identifying colleges and universities that best suit your needs. There are a number of important factors to prepare for when applying for colleges, and one simple task should help you make the most informed choice: research. Without this critical step, it may be extremely difficult to identify the school or schools that fit you the best. Making this decision successfully will change your life forever — for the better!

CHAPTER 3

College — Where Do I Even Start?

The college experience is frightening, intimidating, overwhelming — and exciting, fun, and rewarding all rolled up into one. But before you can even begin to experience life on campus, you have to have a plan to get accepted to that institution. Don't worry; if you have gotten this far along in the book, you're probably on the right track!

Don't waste valuable time worrying if you truly do have the ability to succeed in college. There are many colleges around the country, and there is a college or vocational institution that suits anyone with dreams of higher education. With awfully few exceptions, everyone, if he or she truly wants it, can succeed in college.

Just what do you consider *success*? Some students consider themselves successful if they earn the minimum GPA needed to receive a diploma. Other students, of course, have higher academic expectations. Then there are students who do not measure their success by grades; perhaps their effort has led to an excellent job opportunity immediately after the graduation ceremony, or they have been offered a chance to continue their education at the next level. Although there are certainly some preconceived ideas about the meaning of the word, the bottom line is that you — and you alone — know what you would consider as being successful.

As you may have seen already, even each individual family has an idea of what success means. We have all heard the horror stories of siblings or cousins being matched or pitted against each other for parental expectations or bragging rights. Only you yourself can decide your own definition of success and strive accordingly.

CASE STUDY:

THREE GENERATIONS OF STUDENT "SUCCESS"

I was born in 1935, the youngest of three — and by eight years. My older brother enlisted in the Unites States Marine Corps during WWII, and my older sister took secretarial/stenographer classes and co-op'ed during high school. My brother survived the war and went on to a lifelong career with the United States Army Corps of Engineers and General Services Administration; my sister found steady employment and was paid well (considering the era and the fact she was a woman). None of us went to college at the "normal" age, but we were all "successful."

Later on, after marrying and raising two sons, I felt the urge to take some higher-level classes. When I filled out an application for college, the most difficult part was bridging the gap of the 25 years since I had been graduated from high school. Since this was a two-year school, I do not remember that the requirements were too stringent in the composition department. However, I was able to test out of Freshman English I, II, and III by taking a placement test and scoring in the 97th percentile. The biggest section of that all-day test was written English, including composition, spelling, and grammar.

I eventually earned an Associate's Degree in Library Science, but my career position was as a church Administrative Assistant, where my writing skills were of utmost importance. Most of the letters signed by my supervisor were actually composed by me. Now retired, I presently staff a homework room for intermediate-grade students and am able to be of considerable help to these youngsters with their grammar and spelling. And I also proofread for a widely-circulated monthly Christian periodical, *The Restoration Herald*.

Today's students are not being equipped to write comprehensively. Of my two sons who attended a well-known area college [Miami University of Ohio] in the early 80s, the older one excelled in composition skills and received 4.0 grades in English throughout his college career. The younger had the same English teacher in high school but chose not to avail himself of that ability. Currently, my older son heads up a regional sales division for a major commercial/corporate enterprise. The younger son started working behind the counter at one of the largest fast-food chains during high school and has been a General Manager for that corporation for over 20 years now.

Altogether, I have six grandchildren (and one great-grandchild, but she is too young to be thinking even of kindergarten). My oldest grandson was graduated from Cornell University with honors. In chronological order, the next-oldest works for a fraud investigation firm (he has nearly finished his B.S. in English); the next is a mechanic for an automobile dealership in Nashville ,TN (he graduated from a prestigious automotive school in Nashville with a certificate in bodywork); the next is learning the bakery business in a health food chain (he quit school in his senior year but got a GED). My only granddaughter is currently unemployed, as is her brother — both of whom graduated high school but did not go to college.

— Marilyn Abbott, Administrative Assistant (ret.)
for the Madeira Church of Christ

Talk about how times have changed! In just a couple of generations' time, college (or quality vocational training) has gone from being virtually unnecessary to almost totally essential to find one's way to success in the world — and that everyone has his or her own idea of what that means.

The most important thing to remember when applying to colleges is to have realistic expectations and goals. It goes without saying that the chances of success rapidly diminish if your expectations are unrealistic: do you really expect to hold a 4.0 GPA when you know that math is going to be a real challenge? Sure, there is no harm in trying, but trying and expecting are different.

Developing a set of realistic expectations begins with high school, building a base on which you can build in college. You will need to process what you learn in high school to move on to the next educational level — just as you needed to process from middle-to-high-school and grade-to-middle school. Formal education is designed to be a continual process, with each new level building upon the prior level — but the prior level must be solid and sturdy enough to allow for further construction.

Give yourself a visual: You wouldn't want to place a load of 5,000 pounds on a platform designed to hold only 4,000 and expect it to hold up, right? This would be unrealistic — and foolish!

There are different strategies students use to achieve their college dreams and expectations in a realistic fashion. In simplest terms, you can think of high school as a means to an end; on the other hand, you can think of it as a significant portion of a teenager's life, one that helps you grow and learn — and not just in the academic sense of the word. High school is much more than academic performance; your four years there are filled with pep rallies, sports, proms and homecomings, plays and concerts, and social interactions with other students and the community, all of which contribute to learning in many important ways.

You can think of college as "Grand Central Station" because it merges all that was learned and gained during high school and shapes you into who you will be as an adult — the "you" who wants to climb aboard the College

Express and experience all the scenery along the way as you travel to the destinations you ultimately seek. You are in an important transition period in your life, and you should learn as much as you can from the experience, while adapting to change. There will be some unexpected stops and possible delays along the way, but unless you are completely unprepared or unrealistic in your expectations, there should be no huge train wrecks.

Keep in mind that you have been packing and preparing for this journey for quite a while — at least since eighth grade; it is time to release the brake and proceed.

Your Grades? They're Important!

Let's cut to the chase: yes, elementary school prepared you for junior high school, which in turn prepared you for high school, but preparing for college during the high school years is an ongoing process that requires a significant commitment to your grades. You may be Homecoming King and play in every football game, you may be the female lead in every musical, but colleges and universities will almost always look at academics above all other criteria in the earliest stages of the admission process.

Here are some things to keep in mind when thinking about your grades.

Involve Your Parents

At this high school age and stage of your life, you cannot do all this alone; your parents are the first source of guidance and help. They know you better than anyone else (perhaps even you, for the moment), and if they have taken a proactive interest in grooming you for college, you are already one step ahead of many other students in that your academic performance has been well-nurtured.

One huge way they can help is guiding you to the right classes in high school from one year to the next — something you and your parents should work on together. Stephen Kramer and Michael London address this concept in *The New Rules of College Admissions,* where the authors stress the importance of communication between students and their parents to find the right classes that will be of interest to them as well as challenging. Not only does open communication at home improve the education experience, but a student is more likely to be balanced and satisfied with the high school experience if parents are involved. Both you and your parents need to be open and honest in this ongoing discussion.

Be Honest With Yourself

It is critical to gauge how your academic performance progresses from one year to the next; as you grow, you will change, particularly through the teenage years. Continually assess your own personal strengths and weaknesses, and monitor how they relate to academic performance. Teachers and guidance counselors will also watch your performance and should be able to identify patterns in academic performance and growth or decline in specific subject areas.

Most importantly, if you really want to succeed in college, stay focused on preparing yourself for college-level coursework by choosing high school classes with some degree of difficulty. Find as many options as possible for academic growth through complex and difficult coursework choices — and yet, even at this stage, you don't want to set unrealistic goals. Even in high school, your goals should challenge and push you, but not overwhelm you.

Under license from Shutterstock.com

You will also discover that your skills may be best suited for specific areas of interest, such as the sciences or arts. The terms "left brain" and "right brain" come to mind; we are all wired differently, and we all have different strengths and weaknesses. You may be strong in math, while someone else excels in writing and English, and there is nothing wrong with these differences. Your job is to identify these strengths and to expand upon them as early as possible in high school to develop a specific strategy to grow and reach your educational goals.

Beyond GPA

Even though earning good grades is important, there are other things besides your GPA itself that colleges will consider.

Choosing the Right Classes

Getting good grades is particularly important throughout the junior and senior years. If you select challenging coursework, you look that much better to the college or colleges of your choice, as this indicates you are making an effort to take on a challenging course load, which is necessary in the college environment.

Getting a "B" or better in an accelerated or advanced placement (AP) course is likely to gain positive attention from a college admissions committee over a simpler, easier course in which you earned an "A". The difference lies in the fact that you are willing to accept courses that are not necessarily easy for you to understand and that you are willing to take risks in improving your grades with the potential for a higher GPA.

School Involvement

Throughout high school, it is your responsibility to work hard at your grades, but also be involved in extracurricular activities and your community. Every student is an important part of his or her own school community — some to a higher and more noticeable (and in a positive sense) degree than others; strive to be one of the more visible and active students in your school. Build social skills and meaningful relationships with your teachers and peers; these will also serve a valuable purpose not only in beefing up your application and essays, but give you life-long skills in communication and teamwork.

Working to the Best of YOUR Ability

As a college-bound student, in the classroom and in extracurricular activities, it is your duty to always perform to the best of your ability. Colleges want to see you use your abilities wisely. The ability to expand upon your existing skills and strengths is one of the most important facets of the high school career and is critical to personal development.

Your participation in classes is also important. For some students, getting good grades is practically effortless, but many of them choose not to participate in classroom discussion or extracurricular activities. Admissions committees may not be able to actually observe you participating in your high school classes, but your high school grades will be better for it, and those same teachers may be the ones you ask to write your references later.

Other students also have strong academic ability, yet they have to work extra hard to get good grades. You may find yourself in a similar situation and it can feel exasperating. However, you can gain additional "non-tangible" rewards that aren't shown in a student who excels without any effort — the greatest "non-tangible" being the sense of satisfaction that you did your best work and got that 100 percent.

The key here is to perform to your best ability and to be well-rounded, academically and socially. Showing that you want to work hard and participate will, nine times out of ten, put you in better overall standing than that genius who in reality does not need to strain him/herself and (for whatever reason) remains aloof from the rest.

What If My Grades Aren't the Best?

A word of encouragement: you may be of the less-optimistic mindset that thinks: *My grades will never be good enough for some colleges or universities, so why even try to get better grades?* This is a poor attitude to adopt, as it is more important for you to work hard to improve your grades and show a glimpse of your true academic potential.

Want some inspiration? Remember the movie *Rudy*!

It tells the story of a real-life Notre Dame student who had neither the skills, size, or speed required for college football but always gave a 100 percent effort in the practice squad and refused to be discouraged. For this reason alone, Rudy had the undying loyalty of his Fighting Irish teammates, who threatened to walk out unless he was allowed to play in a real game. No one truly could ever have realistically taken him for a football player, but he was beyond doubt a driven, hard-working overachiever, and for that reason, he was taken seriously as a person.

If you want to attend college, it is your responsibility to make the effort to be taken seriously, not only as a student but also a person because nobody else will do this for you. You control your destiny, and you must be the one to make your college career dreams come true. Your grades matter, but what might ultimately matter more is the determination you showed to achieve them.

To sum it all up, there are many things that make you a good candidate for any college. Your main task is to balance grades with extracurricular activities and social skills to gain entrance into the college of your choice. This is not a simple task, and it may be extremely difficult for you to remain focused throughout this process, particularly when you are unsure as to where you wish to attend college. Nonetheless, focus on your academic performance whenever possible so that your credentials will support your commitment to college achievement. Even if you feel frustrated that you may never know exactly the criteria that the admissions team is looking for, if you possess a serious and steadfast commitment to gaining college acceptance at the school of your choice, you will be more than ready for this challenge — and it will show.

Getting good grades over the long-term is critical, but another important topic relating to grades is standardized testing, which we will discuss in the next chapter.

CHAPTER 4

About the ACT and SAT (EEK!)

So, here you are, enjoying your junior or senior year of high school, enjoying life and your friends as best as you can. Then the inevitable arrives: it is time to take the College Board Standard Assessment Test (SAT) or the American College Testing Program (ACT) and you begin to panic.

You may be nervous regarding what is expected of you. You have most likely taken standardized tests before in elementary or middle school, but those tests never meant as much to you as the grown-up high school version. Standardized tests should be taken seriously, and you should put forth your best effort when the time comes. The SAT and the ACT are an especially important step towards being accepted into the college of your choice.

However. Don't get carried away being worried!

They're Tests — Not the be-all, end-all

This may come as a shock, but not all people who are strong academically perform well on standardized tests. Many students in reality sweat just *thinking* about them, nevermind *taking* them.

But have heart — many students are admitted to college based not so much on SAT or ACT scores; rather, their high school transcripts in general more accurately show their capabilities. Make no mistake — some colleges place more emphasis on these standardized scores than others, and you should take advantage of the practice tests and any study workshops offered at your high school. In the overall scheme of things, you can only prepare yourself as best as possible and (as always) do your absolute best. Standardized test performance largely depends upon your personal and academic ability, which does not follow any particular set of rules.

Despite the scores that you might achieve on standardized tests, there are many issues going on behind the scenes that are bigger than a simple numeric score. For example, colleges and universities looking to admit certain types of applicants are more likely to consider those individuals who obtain the highest scores within the selected applicant pool. The unfortunate reality is that you might perform to the best of your ability during a standardized testing situation, earn an impressive score, and yet fail to impress the admissions committee. They may have seen higher scores from other applicants who might (for whatever reason) be more impressive overall. Don't get discouraged by this bit of news; remember that standardized tests are only a part of the total application process, and that many other criteria are considered.

The standardized test serves many purposes in the college admissions process. Mainly, it determines if you fit the minimum academic criteria for admission, based upon the score(s) that you achieved. Your score also shows an admissions committee how you might fare in their academic programs over the course of your college career. For some colleges, this may serve as a deal-breaker; if you don't fare well on the test, you probably won't gain admission without shining in another area.

Your best course of action to achieve high scores on your standardized tests is to take the PSAT early in the junior year of high school. This test, also known as the Preliminary SAT, is divided into three distinct sections: Math,

Reading, and Writing; in some schools, this test is required. Many guidance counselors recommend that students should take the PSAT test as early as possible in the high school career, as it has a candid ability to predict how you might perform on the SAT and will enable you to prepare more effectively for the real thing. Pay attention during your sophomore year to determine if your school offers the PSAT and if you are eligible to sign up. You want to have as many chances as possible to grow your skills in taking standardized tests early on in high school.

But what do the SAT and ACT really measure? They measure how well you can take the SAT and ACT. They can't measure how smart you are. They can't declare if you're a good student or not. And they certainly don't determine how successful you will be in the future.

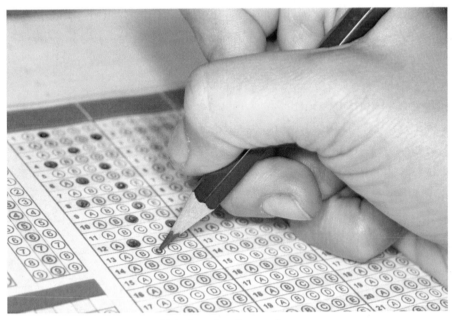

Under license from Shutterstock.com

Standardized tests commonly measure how a student will perform in a pressure-filled situation that is limited by time constraints. This type of scenario is desirable to college admissions experts for a number of reasons, most notably that this situation is likely to assimilate many real-life college testing situations where you have to memorize significant amounts of material in a short period of time. This is particularly important in science- and mathematics-based coursework, although it is useful in other subjects as well. As a result, how you score on the SAT or ACT will serve as a universal guide regarding your ability to convey information in a comparable testing environment. Because testing is an important part of any college setting, admissions committees want to recognize that applicants are actually ready for college classes.

But, on an overall global scale, just how important are your test scores? In *The New Rules of College Admissions,* Kramer and London are quite adamant that colleges look to hold their own academic ranking by admitting only those students who will perform well academically. The standardized tests are a good indication of those who will help keep — or improve — the rankings, and those are the only students who will be accepted.

Even professionals disagree on standardized tests! In *A Is For Admission,* Michelle A. Hernández (a former Dartmouth College Assistant Director of Admissions) re-examined the issue and has changed her opinion over time. Whereas she once felt it was unfair to base a student's future entirely upon a single afternoon's work (compared with the years of education leading up to that afternoon), high school rankings are not always accurately indicative of a student's adaptability to the college realm.

What about class rankings? Some high schools don't even like to use academic rankings because it may encourage unhealthy competition and foster bad feelings among students. But even when students are ranked, high school class rankings don't mean everything. For example, a student who placed first in his graduating class of 50 will rank higher (by the numbers, at least) than one who placed 42nd in a class of over 600. Nevertheless, you have to look at the difficulty of curriculum and the overall capability of the class. Perhaps that number-one student attended a rural, under-funded high school, whose overall curriculum will undoubtedly "lose" when compared with a state-of-the-art, wealthy parochial high school. Still, this young man did graduate number one, and he and four other students will rightfully be able to "pad" their college applications with the fact they placed in the top 10 percent of their class.

Regardless of all the debate, standardized tests are here to stay, and you might as well face the fact you will be taking at least one of them — even if you will never recall anything about it.

What if I Get a Horrible Score?

All right, so let's say you took the test and bombed. Big-time. Although a lower-than-expected standardized test score might seem unfair (you had a really bad sinus headache that day or the car broke down and you barely got there in time), the fact remains that some schools will place more importance on the score than others. Nevertheless, it doesn't seem right to judge a student's ability by that day's examination. The perceived "strengths and weaknesses" (particularly the weaknesses) on that given day may be misleading in the overall scheme of things so far as you are concerned. And yet, this can be the case, so you must be prepared.

A sign of maturity is how you respond to challenges. This may perhaps be the most important factor in showing your ability to succeed in college. Rather than giving up and stressing that you won't make it into your chosen college, just adjust your plan. There are many schools out there, and you will have other chances to perform better on future tests. Try again, keep your options open and you will eventually find the best overall fit.

Although standardized testing may be difficult for some, they are simple for others, and more often than not, these are the students also excel academically in most subject areas. Of course, what standardized tests can't show are the other aspects of a developing college-bound student. This is where good high school transcripts can also fill in the blanks. Unlike mere report cards, the progression of classes and grades as reflected there reveal more information overall than any given day's test results.

Let's also not forget that how you perform once you are in college will be a further reflection of your overall character and chances for success; if you apply yourself, those test scores and other academic standards will almost certainly rise further than you might have imagined — even if you are not "genius" material.

Here is a terrific example, from one student who might not have been happy with his test score at first.

CASE STUDY:

THE FIRST IN LINE

I was excited to go to college because nobody else in my family ever had. I had also seen co-workers at dead-end jobs who were not going anywhere and probably never would. When I first decided to go to college, I initially was going to enroll in a community college and just be satisfied with a two-year Associate's Degree. It was shortly after I graduated from high school that I decided to go to a university and get a four-year Bachelor's Degree with the intention of continuing on to graduate school

I knew I wanted to stay close to home, so I began to look at local schools. My first choice was the University of Cincinnati. After contemplating exactly what I wanted to major in, I decided to apply at Northern Kentucky University. Within a few short days of applying, I received a letter in the mail congratulating my acceptance and also a congratulatory phone call from the university. I was now enrolled as a full time student majoring in Computer Science.

Before applying to any university, I had to take one of many exams in order to get accepted. I choose to take the ACT while still in my senior year in high school. Preparing for the ACT was a simple process, due to the amount of available material and prep courses. However, after the test was taken and the results were in, I was by no means pleased with the score that I got. I decided to retake the exam, this time getting much higher than the first but not exactly what I wanted.

Although my score was high enough to get into NKU, I personally was not pleased. But I decided to let it go and not really bother me because although my score was not the top, I knew I would be okay.

I just finished my second year at NKU, and am currently on the Dean's List, aided by a 4.0 GPA in my third semester. Since the beginning, I have changed majors twice and finally decided to finish out my Bachelor's Degree double-majoring in Construction Management and Construction Technology. Deciding to go to a university was the best decision that I have ever made.

Although my ACT score was not what I wanted it to be, the two years that I have been at NKU have proven to me that I can do anything that I want to do — all I have to do is set my mind to it.

— Justin Thompson, Student, Northern Kentucky University

As you can see, standardized test results are not the end-all; you don't have to "kiss your college dreams goodbye." Even so, when taking standardized tests it's best to perform to the best of your ability and develop the best opportunities for success. The cold, hard fact is that these test scores are taken into consideration for virtually every college or university. Grit your teeth through that headache, take non-drowsy sinus relief medication, forget about the car for these next few hours, and give this test all you have because it <u>will</u> matter. This may be an unfortunate circumstance, but it clearly demonstrates that overall academic performance — in transcripts and testing — is an important aspect of your college admissions plan.

CHAPTER 5

Did Someone Say, "Options"?

Let's go over what we've discussed thus far. You have self-reflected, talked with your parents, teachers, and counselors, and have decided that you definitely want to go to college. You've started thinking about what kind of college might interest you and listed your most basic priorities, you have taken the standardized tests, and — most important of all — you have truly "buckled down" to make the most of your remaining high school days, both grade-wise and socially.

Researching Your Options

At the advice of your guidance counselor, you have gotten a clearer idea of when and how to begin the application process. You've also begun some online research and sent off for information from various institutions that caught your interest, and the mailbox is overstuffed — perhaps even with some basic information from schools (postcards, single-page flyers) you did not actively request but that somehow found out that you are college-shopping — ahhh, the wonders of modern technology!

What should you do with all of the information you're receiving — paper or electronic — from colleges? Stay organized! Obviously you will save items from the colleges you're most interested in to look it over later, but you need to create a system to keep yourself from getting overwhelmed.

You want to keep information handy, but you don't have to save everything; remember that today's technology will allow you to quickly find anything you need with a quick phone call or internet search. If you are a saver (or your parents are the type that don't throw anything away), an idea could be to purchase an expandable file to sort and organize physical papers from colleges, and take time to create folders and sub-folders in your email account for electronic information.

While searching, you might feel that the choices are overwhelming. Private against public, liberal arts against specialty, pre-med or pre-law against mathematics, large against small; the list goes on. For each of these options, you need to look at a variety of criteria, and it is important to always be working from the list you already began to narrow down your college application choices.

Hopefully, the colleges you're looking at have already been taken from that first list of priorities discussed in Chapter 2: for example, if it's important for you to be by the beach, you probably shouldn't have requested information from the University of Nebraska.

The Search Is On

But now what? You asked for information from several colleges and they (and five more that weren't on your radar) have responded. How do you begin to narrow down your list? There are many options to help you find the best course of action that plays to your personal strengths and needs.

How many schools should I research?

For some students, the college application experience is pretty simple; they may have only two schools in mind when they begin the process, with one far and above the other, and upon gaining acceptance to both, the choice is made almost immediately. For most students however, this process is not frequently so cut-and-dry; many colleges are piquing their interest, and so it is often really difficult to narrow down the list.

Let's say you're not one of the lucky ones with only two options. You've looked at many colleges, studying their brochures and poring over their websites. How many of these should you apply? According to *The New Rules of College Admission,* the ideal number should be seven; authors Kramer and London break down this figure into a 2:3:2 ratio, with the first two being ideal, the middle three being just right, and the last two being adequate for your needs. You may consider this to number to be too small or too large, but the idea is help you narrow your choices while still giving some latitude.

If you like sports (and if you don't, bear with us), picture the "March Madness" of NCAA basketball. Over 60 teams start off in the tournament (with half of them eliminated immediately), and the brackets gradually work their way down to Sweet 16, Elite Eight, Final Four, and then the championship game. Now, no one expects you to have investigated 60 schools (if you did, um, wow!), but the truth is that like any truly "weak" team that somehow found its way into the tourney, many of the colleges that originally appealed to you will immediately be discarded, for one reason or other. Picturing the "Elite Eight" is closest to what you should consider for applying, and if all eight colleges accept you, you may have to go through your own version of the Final Four before deciding the champion.

Keep your focus

Eliminate colleges and universities that don't align with your own criteria and key strengths. For example, if your high school GPA is 3.2, you probably won't be looking at an Ivy League school like Harvard or Yale. It's not wise to waste time researching a college or university that does not fit your knowledge and skill-set.

It's all about the money, money, money

Let's face it: money is a concern for most of us. You need to look at the financial cost of college, especially when comparing public to private colleges and universities. If you decide on a public university located in your home state, the tuition rate is likely to be much lower than at an out-of-state institution.

If you happen to live in an area near a state border, there may be a "reciprocity" agreement; for instance, the states of Minnesota and Wisconsin have an agreement, as stated here:

"Under the reciprocity program, any student who is enrolled in an eligible program and meets residency requirements at a public university in Wisconsin may attend a Minnesota public institution on a space available basis and pay the established reciprocity tuition charges for course work that is located in Minnesota." [2]

Reciprocity can mean transferring of grades, financial costs, or both; there is a mutual agreement between these colleges to accept each other's students with no additional "out-of-state" charges added to tuition costs.

Your best option is to research the costs associated with taking a full-course load, along with books and other fees, and then to decide if you will live on campus or if you live close enough to commute from home to class. (Of course, depending on gas prices, either choice could save you money over the long term, depending on how close you are from school.)

---

2. http://heab.state.wi.us/docs/reciprocity/mnwi1617.pdf, 2017

Most college students will live in a dormitory, at least to start out, and some eventually live in apartments near campus. You need to be realistic about the additional cost of living you will have. What do the dorms cost, and what is included in those fees (food, parking)? How reasonable, clean, and safe are the apartments? Room and board costs might be an important part of the financial picture of going to college, so research all of your options early in the game.

Classes and majors that fit your needs

There are a number of factors you will look at for each college, including class offerings, class size, and overall academic strengths within your selected major — or the best programs for undecided-at-present majors. Will you get a variety of different class types you need — lecture or discussion types, or even labs? Weighing and comparing all these factors may seem particularly daunting at first; though, once you have pared the number of colleges down to a select few, the evaluations will become easier.

Extra-curricular activities

Of course, there is more to college than the classes. Do you like drama, plays, or improv? Are you artistic? Do you like to volunteer, or is there a hobby you want to explore? Whether you play sports, are musical, or want to get involved in student government, college has activities for everyone! Every college website should have information about all of the different activities offered. It is also helpful to talk with faculty and students to find out if your interests are represented. These can lead to scholarships — or add to the fun of a well-rounded college experience.

Avoid Procrastinating!

This whole process might seem like it is taking forever. Researching colleges might take some time, and even after you have applied, the wait might be long. But the worst mistake you can make is to procrastinate. The decisions you are making will affect the rest of your life and you need to take them seriously. Making a wise choice requires the ability to analyze, evaluate, and absorb a large amount of information over time; the sooner you begin, the better. Don't expect to "wing it" at the last minute or read ten different packets in one afternoon; start the process as soon as possible and allow yourself time to fully look over all the research.

It's important to remember that you're not the only student who is college-bound! You're not the only one whom colleges have contacted, and there are many more who would be willing to take your place — and some of them (believe it or not) won't procrastinate. If you truly want to go to college, and have an opportunity to apply for and be admitted to the school of your choice, don't waste any time.

Don't worry; you are well on your way, and you are really not as "alone" as it may seem. I highly urge that you talk about your frustrations and concerns with your parents, teachers, guidance counselors, and friends so that you will be better able to further winnow down which college will be appropriate for you.

Although you alone can make the final decision, simply talking things over with someone else — having a fresh "ear" to listen to your concerns — may ease the confusion. Someone else might be able to offer a whole new perspective or solution that clarifies things. There is an old saying about not being able to see the forest through the trees — well, a fresh opinion or suggestion just may chop down a few trees and make that forest seem less formidable.

Under license from Shutterstock.com

CASE STUDY:

AT THE CROSSROADS

I applied to several universities while I was a senior at an all girls' college prep academy in Cincinnati, Ohio. I decided to only apply to five colleges due to the fact that I did not want to go too far from home, but I also did not want to stay in-state. I, with my senioritis setting in, also did not want to have to take the SAT II, which some universities required for their application. Therefore, I applied to Purdue, Indiana University, Marquette University, Emory University, and Washington University in St. Louis, and I did get into all five schools. I finally decided to attend Washington University due to their excellent pre-medical biology program, overall reputation, and gorgeous campus. I also decided to run on their varsity track and field team.

As I recall, the most difficult part of the application was writing the essay! The essay usually asks you to talk about some aspect of your personality or your career goals. As an 18-year-old, I was not exactly sure what I wanted to do with my life. I began thinking about what had impacted me the most in my life so far, and what things I truly enjoyed doing.

Overall, I think that the most challenging part of writing any essay is the introduction. I have a difficult time writing an introductory sentence that captures the audience, but also conveys what the subject of my paper will be. I usually start by making a list of ideas, terms, and phrases that come to mind when I think about the subject of my essay. This gets my thought process going and prevents me from leaving anything out of the essay. I start by writing a little about each idea that I came up with, and eventually I connect those ideas to each other in order to make the essay flow.

Although I do not write often, I find writing to be cathartic. Whether it is writing an email to a friend or journaling about an event in my life, I find that writing enables me to get my feelings out on paper and think more clearly. I think that being able to write and express oneself is very important especially when it comes to applying for jobs, graduate school, or even just to communicate with others. I feel that writing skills are a reflection of one's personality, style, creativity, personal experiences, and education.

— Valerie Lasko, Research Assistant,
University of Cincinnati College of Medicine

Valerie was able to use the same essay for all five applications, making the process easier for her. This isn't always the case — hope for the best but prepare for the worst.

In conclusion to this chapter, here is a Case Study from Valerie's brother, whose college application and acceptance were far less stressful; he had only one choice that appealed to him, and there was no written application.

CASE STUDY:

(ALMOST) NO WRITING REQUIRED

I sent written application to only one college, DeVry University. DeVry was founded in Chicago Illinois. There are now campuses all over the United States from coast-to-coast. DeVry is a four-year institution that awards Associate and Bachelor degrees. They now have Master's Level programs in Business and Technology.

The application was easy. The recruiter came to my school and then met with my parents and me at our house. I was accepted to DeVry in Columbus, Ohio almost right away. I received a Bachelor of Science degree in 2007 majoring in Computer Engineering Technology.

There was never any question that my skills were in the area of mathematics and computers. I even attended a vocational and technical high school in Cincinnati, Ohio that allowed me to capitalize on my strengths. Writing was never my forte: I knew early on in my education that I was writing-challenged when it came to book reports and essays. Even the shortest assignments seemed too long.

Many teachers and instructors tried to encourage me, but none succeeded. I just did not like to write. I found that "hands-on" activities and assignments were more rewarding. I have mechanical skills and enjoy building engines and working on cars. Computers always fascinated me, so I chose a college that would enhance and develop my technical abilities.

I have to admit that writing skills are more important than I thought now that I am employed as a systems analyst for a large corporation. I write official emails on a daily basis, so I have to be able to express myself well. But hey, at least they're not as long as those school assignments!

Richard S. Lasko, Systems Analyst

CHAPTER 6

Selecting Students — A College's "Write"

S o far we've been talking about getting into college from the student's point of view. In this chapter, we're going to change our viewpoint and think about it from the college's perspective.

In some aspects, the way a college selects its future students has remained fairly standard over the course of time, but — especially within the past 50-or-so years — there have been many new developments that can both help and hinder the whole process. The most obvious of these developments: computer technology. It's resulted in better ways of managing databases (student transcripts and standardized testing) and helped make research easier for projects and essays. However, some people think that technology has the potential to make the modern student "lazy," especially when it comes to writing.

Colleges are Businesses Investing in Their Students

Colleges and universities have an idea of the kind of student they want, based on a variety of different criteria at each individual school. As a prospective student, your responsibility is to identify these criteria and determine if you are a good fit for their school. It's a tough concept to swallow, but you must also consider the fact that colleges seek to admit only the most qualified applicants for their programs, and — current writing levels notwithstanding — colleges are just getting more picky and exclusive in recent years.

All colleges and universities — Ivy League, public, private, and community — want those students who are most likely to succeed, as this reflects the college itself. With the number of higher-education institutions growing every year, there is increased competition among them for strong student candidates (a.k.a. good, well-rounded potential alumni) to help a college or university keep a good reputation.

Colleges and universities are businesses. And like any business, they want only the best ingredients or materials to make a final product that encourages more people to buy in the future. After all, as with any enterprise, they need good results to increase their chances of being able to stay in business. It's just not logical for a college to admit a student with a poor GPA and a flimsy record of accomplishment — or one who shows a definite weakness in — or, perhaps more than a definite weakness, an *obvious dislike* for writing.

Wait — that's still not a good way to phrase it; let's try this: an *obvious dislike of wanting to improve* at writing. Having less-than-stellar writing skills is something you can work on; you are applying to college to learn and to improve yourself. You may never love writing, but as you have no doubt heard from your parents and teachers, there will always be things you have to do that you would rather not.

Even as you invest in applying to a college, that college or university must also weigh the advantages of investing in its applicants. Good writing skills, and even more so the willingness to build upon them, are a strong indicator to the college that you really are an "ingredient" that may benefit their final product — which, after all, includes you. Believe it or not, even more than the school-logo sweatshirt or ball cap you wear, your skills in the real world just may be the best advertisement for the institution — and they will be one of your best-selling when you go to offer yourself to a future employer.

Under license from Shutterstock.com

CASE STUDY:

MY LOVE/HATE RELATIONSHIP WITH WRITING

What was the most challenging part of making your college application?

The most apprehension I felt in the application process was the acknowledgement that my grades were not above average and my writing skills were below par. Despite the confidence I now have after several years' experience in college, I remember that writing the application essays was a difficult process.

Knowing that you are among those who do not like to write (essays or otherwise), what is the most challenging part of writing and how do you overcome it?

There seems to be a block in my mind. When I look at a blank page or a blank screen, I become overwhelmed with anxiety. It used to be unbearable. Now, after having to write so many papers in college, it has become easier.

I find that initially when having to write, it is good to sit down and discuss how you feel and what you are thinking about the topic with a friend or loved one. I find that it is easy for me to verbally describe my thoughts and feelings but challenging to put into print. After talking about the topics with people, I suggest writing down facts and ideas on the paper while even ignoring the lines. Afterwards you can elaborate from there.

Oftentimes, I have verbalized my thoughts and had someone else type them using my words. Later, I would go back and reorganize. In the beginning, you might need someone to help you put the thoughts together in a fluid manner. The road to writing does get easier. It will never be a walk in the park, but it definitely gets smoother. Even just having a study-buddy, mentor or warm body to be there physically can help you stifle the anxiety enough to write. Just write. Throw it all up on paper and edit later.

Pretend for a minute that you like to write; what gratification do you find, and what is your favorite kind of writing?

The finished product is the most amazing part. Handing over that complete work, knowing that I have completed a task is the most pleasing to me. I find that it is most gratifying and easiest to write about is my personal life experiences and inner feelings. They tend to be the most captivating samples, too.

Have you ever had a composition instructor, either in high school or early college, who really "turned you off" to writing? How did he/she do this?

No, actually most of my instructors have tried to encourage and challenge me to be a good writer. I have simply disliked it on my own.

Have you ever had a composition instructor who helped you "discover" the rewards of writing?

It is plain and simple that I do not like to write. Although I have had wonderful instructors, it is an innate thing in me to dislike writing. I have distractibility issues among other things. While I feel as though that through my experiences I have become a better writer I still do not like to write.

Do you feel that writing skills have proven important throughout your post-college life/career?

I am still in college. But my friend Anna, who is a teacher, tells me every day how important writing is in her profession. She told me once that her superior would write emails that contained misspelled words, un-capitalized, and un-punctuated sentences. It seemed to her that the message was taken less seriously, in addition to the respect that is lost for someone who is being paid more than you and has to handle more official responsibilities. Plus, as a teacher you have to set a good example. You do not want to teach your students mistakes that will duplicate over time.

— Pam Lasko, Student, Wright State University

Here is a student who admits to disliking writing, yet who applied to three colleges (remember her story in Chapter 1?) and was accepted by all three; here is a student who still feels that writing is not her "thing" and yet has learned how to successfully navigate the waves; and — most importantly — here is a student who grits and grinds her way through every essay assignment, but who recognizes the value of representing herself through the written word, both at college and in the professional world.

Different Colleges, Different Requirements

So, how much does your written application really matter when applying to the college of your choice? We've been stressing the high value of writing: the truth is that some colleges will hold this to be more important than others.

For example, a technical college such as the one attended by a future systems analyst probably won't require the degree of writing skills equivalent to a Liberal Arts college application. Even so, the better the written application, the more appealing the student will look to an admissions officer because strong writing skills reflect an overall ability to learn, grasp and — most importantly — use what you've learned. Even if your chosen career is in systems programming and software design, don't forget that other students are hoping for the same career course and are applying just like you are.

It's safe to assume that, even in such a techno-centric institution, writing skills just might be the "tiebreaker" when it comes to making final selection as to which students will be admitted. All other things being equal (such as GPA, achievements, social activities, and so on), the student with a better chance is the one who can best express himself or herself in that application essay — even if it didn't seem so important at the time it was written.

Remember that in your job later in life, there is a good chance that you may have to write memos or instructions to employers, fellow employees, and/or customers using your company's systems. Even if this type of writing is more of what is termed technical writing, the most basic technical writing will reflect on you and your overall ability to do a good job. Rightly or wrongly, careless writing reflects on your overall capabilities — and those admissions officers will be able to see that long before your potential employers or clients in four years' time.

And there still are other majors where high-quality writing is a major part of the studies. You might be picturing those writing tasks (and dreading them) when you think of college . . . the research, the formal quotations, footnotes and endnotes and citations (oh, my), the argumentative essays — in other words, the "non-technical-writing writing." It goes without saying that the writing skills and the effort put forth in an application essay at Dartmouth will hold more weight than at a technical college; even though the application essay for the latter was a "tiebreaker," some colleges will use this essay as the first thing they look at as soon as minimum GPA and other basic criteria have been revealed.

BUT . . . Relax!

At this point, you may need some reassurance. You've been reading about all the challenges you're are going to face and how you must excel and apply yourself and all that rah-rah intellectual hype. The bells are ringing in your head and the academic clock is about ready to chime. Yes, all that is true, but it is not an education death-knell; you are going to be fine.

You are still young!

Don't forget that you are a young adult entering a whole new phase of life and its challenges. Colleges and universities recognize the importance of these challenges and the need for students to adapt to new circumstances while honing skills and strengths. They also want students to understand that higher education enables academic growth and excellence and that new forms of knowledge will serve as a starting point for a professional career.

You can still grow!

Colleges and universities want you to work and study hard, but also to enjoy the time that is spent there. You will discover how the college years will provide a strong, firm foundation for the future. Your job as a college student is to take those opportunities and develop them as best as you can into as many memorable and educational experiences as possible.

You can still develop skills!

Of course colleges want students with good grades and academic skills; yet, they also are looking for students with lots of different experiences, including extracurricular activities. These activities might include team sports, community service, clubs, and part-time jobs. Fraternities, sororities, and other on-campus organizations will offer an array of social and professional networking opportunities; all of these experiences will help promote a well-rounded individual who has the potential for success throughout life.

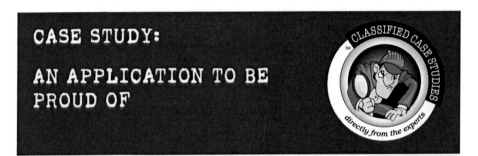

CASE STUDY:

AN APPLICATION TO BE PROUD OF

As a high school English teacher for many years, I have helped a number of students write college application essays. At its most fundamental level, the college application essay process is fairly simple and only requires students to be praising of themselves. The most difficult challenge is finding a balance between humility and self-praise. The student needs to laud his or her accomplishments, but at the same time make note of the fact that he or she needs the college to which they are applying to further hone their talents. This is a key element to the essay process. The student must show that he or she is able to be taught and desires such. If this balance is struck, then the applicant will be in good shape so far as the admissions committees are concerned.

In general, a good college-applicant resume-builder is service work, or any work that deals with justice. However, this work should not be done just to pad that resume. A sincere devotion to justice (or lack of same) will come across in any college application essay. Sincerity is key; colleges want an honest and dedicated individual who can show he or she has committed to something for a period of time. Service work, particularly long-term, shows that an individual is committed and caring, which is a very attractive trait to any college administrator.

To bring things into a more personal perspective, I moderate a group of students, M.A.C.H. 1 (Moeller Advocates for Community Housing), who seek to provide affordable housing for Cincinnati's indigent. Working mainly in the part of town known as "Over-the-Rhine," I and my crew have stripped vacant and decrepit buildings down to their bare skeletons and then re-modeled/refurbished them in order to give otherwise-homeless inner city people a chance to get off the streets and have a roof over their heads.

This experience is most helpful in preparing students for college, as it teaches them leadership, time management and a myriad of practical life skills. Sending altruistic students to college betters the college campus and has a profound ripple effect on all whom come in contact with the student. Additionally, colleges look highly upon individuals with experience in justice work, as justice is the most honorable goal for which anyone can strive.

— Mike Moroski, English Department, Moeller High School

To finish out this chapter, colleges and universities do not just look for students who satisfy their academic requirements; they also want to *develop* prospective students and their ambitions. Obviously, students who are willing to get their hands dirty and help those in need already show promise as people who will apply themselves to any worthwhile cause — including themselves. If you can present yourself as one who is confident and willing to grow to further develop yourself all-around, you will undoubtedly score high in the committee's favor.

Take note: admissions officers are not there to help you learn/improve your writing skills (that will be done by your professors). Admissions workers will be looking first at how your written work reflects <u>you</u> and not so much (at this stage) your writing skills, although — just as with your grades and standardized testing — it never hurts to do your best in both.

CHAPTER 7

What Do They REALLY Want to See in My Essay?

f you're this far into the college admission process, you already know that you'll probably have to write an essay, or even several essays, as part of applying. You may be wondering what they'll be about. The essays could cover several topics like personal career aspirations, strengths and weaknesses, and other personal matters. It's also typical to find several required questions, in addition to one or more optional questions, for consideration. As a college applicant, it's your responsibility to read these questions carefully and to determine how to address them in the most appealing way.

Colleges like seeing essays that are complete and precise, but also aren't too wordy or filled with "fluff" without any true substance. There are many books available that offer examples of good, "winning" essays (you can check out the bibliography at the end of this book for a few), and you might want to read over at least a handful so you can get the feel of how your essays should sound.

Under license from Shutterstock.com

Generally . . .

They Want to See Some Effort

Teachers and admissions officers can tell pretty quickly which students are really making an effort (despite the occasional but inevitable technical issue) to express themselves well on paper, and which ones are too lazy to even make an effort. It is also readily apparent which students are going to ramble on forever just trying to cover the minimum page length requirement. All quantity, no quality — embarrassingly obvious to both writer and reader — is not the way to go.

They Want to Learn About You

Perhaps the most important first step to developing a successful admissions essay is to bear in mind that you are writing about yourself, in your own words. You shouldn't make these words so mind-numbing that readers will find your story and life history the most boring piece of information on earth. Take pride in showing that your story is no less interesting or fascinating than anybody else's story. That being said, you should develop your opinions and thoughts as creatively as possible and try to make the ordinary sound endearing.

Keep in mind that there are indeed limits to the type and extent of information that you reveal about yourself in the essay (you've heard the phrase T.M.I — too much information). Your words should be honest and real, but still recognizable as a part of what you represent. Therefore, you should only reveal details that will sell your story to the admissions committee and that will promote a sense of understanding and empathy towards your character. You want them to read your essay and say to themselves, *Now this is the type of student who belongs at our college. He or she represents a strong character, and will show a commitment to his or her academic studies.*

Make it authentic. Look at this Case Study example written -by a pharmaceutical major, then compare it to the drastically different one that follows which was submitted by a lifelong Humanities college professor.

CASE STUDY:

I DID NOT REALLY FRET OVER MY COLLEGE ADMISSIONS ESSAY

When I was applying for college, I sent written applications to Ohio State University, Ohio Northern University, the University of Cincinnati and the University of Toledo. I selected these institutions because they offered my selected major, Pharmacy, and they were all in-state schools.

To me, the most challenging part of writing any college application essay was coming up with content or a story that will really score with the college admissions team. One of the hardest parts of drafting my applications was the random essay question, when one was required. I found it easier when I was given at least some idea of what to write. I did not ask anyone for help, and did not have any help other than from a dictionary or thesaurus.

When it comes to impressing admissions faculty I would tell applicants to think of the best situation in their life that applies to the question. Do not lie or make up extraordinary situations to make yourself sound greater than you are. Just pick a normal example of whatever the admissions faculty is asking about — but it is always a bonus if you can throw in points about being a leader, service in the community, or some other good quality.

— Amanda Gray, University of Toledo

And here is a completely different perspective.

CASE STUDY:

HOW IMPORTANT IS WRITING IN THE DECISION TO ACCEPT A STUDENT AT A COLLEGE?

I believe the application essay is a crucial element in the acceptance process. All the data that students submit — grade point averages, transcripts, extracurricular activities and so on — can be misleading, because the reader cannot be sure exactly what is being measured, or against what standard. Even standardized test scores tell more about the socioeconomic status of the student's parents than about the student's specific abilities.

But the application essay gives the college a chance to hear the student's individual voice. This voice reveals something about the student's verbal ability (though the reader must always allow for the possibility that the student has had help polishing the essay), but more importantly, the essay reveals aspects of the student's personality which cannot be quantified — like how the student thinks, how she perceives the world, what her priorities are, what values he offers to the college community. The essay, in other words, is a place where the student can distinguish her/himself from all the other super-achievers she is competing with.

Let me use my three stepsons as examples: three young men, all academically gifted, but with very different personalities and talents. They used their application essays to reveal something unexpected about themselves, something not to be found in their list of school achievements and extracurricular activities.

The oldest wrote about the shock he experienced when, in the ninth grade, he moved from a Montessori school to a traditional high school. In contrast to the more individualized assignments and process-based evaluations he had known for eight years, he encountered highly structured classes and frequent grades. It was quite a shock, and at first he was not very successful in this new environment. But he used his intellect to analyze the new expectations and figured out ways to meet them, and soon was as successful as his new school as he had been at his old one. This story revealed the struggles of a confident young man experiencing failure for the first time in his life; his success indicated his ability to face challenges. But more importantly, the voice of the essay which was self-aware, humorous, and wry offered significant information about th quality of his mind. Any admissions officer reading this essay would have a strong sense of this student as a person, more than any transcript or test score could convey.

The second young man traced his choice of academic specialty, Eastern Asian languages and cultures, to his encounter at 14 with an animated version of The Romance of the Three Kingdoms, an ancient Chinese novel about war and politics. The world revealed by the film so fascinated him that he not only read three different translations of this thousand-page work, but created a small club of like-minded students at his high school. His essay examined the values he found in this culture and analyzed how those values might provide meaning for his life in the very different context of modern American society. By focusing on a story that was unique to him, and by articulating the significance of this story in a voice that was unmistakably his own, he provided an admissions officer with a valuable clue to the qualities he would offer the college.

The third, rather than focusing on his career goals of medical school, chose to write about an unusual achievement that he prided himself on: every day for the last two years of high school, he rode his bicycle to school, a hilly five-mile trip each way, carrying a backpack nearly half his body weight, undeterred by any variety of inclement weather. This feat, and the motivations for it, revealed a number of important things about his character: his determination, his desire for independence, his concern for the environment, and his delight at being different from virtually all of his fellow students. His transcripts and test scores testified to his academic abilities, but in the essay, he offered the admissions officers access to those other qualities a student can bring to the table.

What each of these essays had in common is that they approached the assignment from an unexpected angle. Each young man chose to emphasize an aspect of himself other than academic ability or career goals, to tell a story about who he was and where he was coming from, and in a voice that revealed the self behind the numbers (and each young man was successful in gaining admission to his first-choice school). That's what a good college application essay needs to do.

— Kathleen L. Spencer, Ph.D

It is certainly a "no-brainer" to spot the differences between these two Case Studies, but they both reflect a good example of what we discussed: how important your essay is to your admission can vary, depending upon which school and what type of college courses you will take. Although Ms. Gray has somewhat downplayed her effort, the truth is that a future pharmacologist/pharmacist will not have to write on the same level, or style, as an aspiring foreign-language major (conversely, the foreign-language major will not have to memorize the Periodic Table of the Atomic Elements). But what these Case Studies do have in common is that all four of the students in the examples got into their schools of choice — and they all had to write an essay.

What to Include

You, too, can have a rocking college admissions essay. Let's look at some of the fundamentals, most of which you've probably been hearing since you started doing book reports in grade school.

A Thesis / Introduction

You have to start somewhere, and your main idea is a great place to start. Decide on your thesis (don't let that nasty word scare you — let's instead call it a "mission statement" if it makes you feel better) and what you want to say to support that statement. You have something to say, and a reason you want to say it; all that should come through as your essay develops. By the end, you will have introduced, expounded upon, and concluded your mission, which has with any luck enraptured your audience and show off your capabilities.

A Good English Teacher's Advice on Essays? They have three parts: 1. Tell 'em what you're gonna tell 'em, 2) Tell 'em, and 3) Tell 'em what you told 'em.

The beginning of your essay shouldn't open with a lengthy, dull opening sentence. This type of introduction will get you nowhere fast — other than possibly to the "reject" pile. If your reader has to look back and re-read several times just to get the idea, your essay is doomed. Craft an introductory sentence and an opening paragraph that addresses who you are and what you represent as quickly as possible. If you develop a strong introductory sentence and paragraph, the remainder of your essay should naturally flow and lead to a successful body and conclusion.

Consider the following student whose literary skills were 'eh' at best, but whose essays were among the most powerful any Language Arts teacher ever read. Coming as he did from a rundown inner-city area, his papers could have easily started off along this line (with the spelling, punctuation, and grammar cleaned up a bit):

I'd always wondered what it felt like to be shot.

Instead, his style was far grittier and eye-catching:

Bang. I fell into the stairwell. My ears rang and my leg and side burned like hell. The concrete was cold. I tried to get up, but felt numb.

Immediately, the reader can guess much about the author; he has been shot, seems to be in a cold, tough neighborhood, and despite pain and numbness, has the presence of mind to try to recover. Compare this with the first selection, where all we know is that the author has a weird curiosity of bullet wounds. We don't know whether he or she ends up getting shot, or knowing someone who gets shot, and more to the point, his/her curiosity does nothing to truly set him/her apart from most of us who, at one time or another, have probably wondered the same thing.

Your opening statement should be authentic, demonstrating why you as a prospective student would be successful at the college of your choice. There are countless ways to approach this, such as with humor, conviction, gumption, or even sadness or fear; no matter which approach that you take, show that you are sincere. Your words are meaningless unless you write them from your heart. Admissions readers can tell the difference.

Bear in mind that you want to make your first sentence glow and appear alive as best as you can. As the old saying goes, *You don't get a second chance to make a first impression*, so you should write to impress right off the bat. A creative and catchy first sentence and paragraph will lead you down the right path for the remainder of your essay. Yet, if you feel you must start with a "safe" first sentence, follow it with a catchy phrase or statement that will attract the reader's attention: *I always wondered what it felt like to be shot. Forget curiosity - it hurts worse than anything I've ever felt and I cannot move to tell them not to throw me in that ambulance.*

This process is not rocket science, and frankly, it's not that different from writing an essay for a high school English class. You've just served up an appetizer and salad for your audience; now, the meat and potatoes of the essay must be filling, followed by a dessert that leaves a good taste in the reader's confidence in you as a student. You've been hearing this recipe in some form throughout your schooling, and probably have been doing it, even when you weren't aware of it, as your writing skills have improved.

A Body that Matches Your Introduction in Tone, Style, and Content

Let's assume that you've written the introduction of your life. It's not too wordy, it's creative, it's heartfelt, it's funny, and it describes your personality to a tee. What now? How do you follow through and keep the remainder of the essay strong?

The most important thing to remember in this process is to remain focused. Without a clear focus, your essay is likely to become a rambling mess — just as when you verbally relate a story but allow too many side comments and distractions. Do your best to develop the body in the same way you developed the introduction: with flair and finesse. Your commitment to the essay as a whole is what will keep you on track and keep your message clear.

Because you've already established a specific tone in your introduction, your best bet is to hold that tone throughout the remaining paragraphs. If you continue to write with the same tone and style, your attention to the project will be obvious to the Admissions Committee who will be more likely to view your essay positively. Plus, your demonstration of well-directed and controlled creative energy will remain strong, thought-provoking, and sincere.

A good example can be found in the gunshot wound essay from before. There is a powerful, attention-grabbing introduction, but the tone of the essay must remain consistent throughout. Reread the opening and think of one of those old black-and-white detective movies, where the narrator speaks tersely and pulls no verbal punches: *Bang. I fell into the stairwell. My ears rang and my leg and side burned like hell. The concrete was cold. I tried to get up, but felt numb.* The speaker is abrupt, to the point, and maintains a sort of sarcastic sneer that echoes in his delivery and choice of words.

No matter how brilliant the introduction, that essay would have been ruined, shot through the heart, and bleeding in the stairwell right along with its author, if he had suddenly sounded soft-hearted: *I found myself thinking about my beloved Angie, and how she had always begged me not to come down this street after dark. Oh, how I wish I had listened.* Not only does this clash in the reader's ear, sabotaging the picture that was previously formed of the author's character, but it also shows an inability to stay on a set course.

A Conclusion to Make an Impact

After you've written the introduction and body of your essay, finish your work like you began. Often, it's good to round off with a nod to the introduction: *"I will never wonder again what it feels like to be shot; I now know,"* (as in the first example) — or, for the second and better example: *"My leg's still sore and I have lost some blood, but what the hell I'll live."*

If you began the essay with a humorous tone, you should conclude the same way. This approach will at least prove that you're consistent and that, in spite of the essay's humor bookends (intro and conclusion), you've taken your mission seriously. On the other hand, if you wrote the essay with a serious tone, don't end it with a joke. Again, the tone of the essay should remain consistent throughout — right up to the final punctuation mark. The conclusion is as important as the introduction and more or less wraps things up. It may also be what the committee remembers most when recalling your submission.

If your essay tells your life story or a specific phase of it, end on a positive note, along with a few statements that reaffirm who you are, what you represent, and how you might develop and grow further through the college experience you're seeking. The admissions committee will appreciate a positive approach which should work really favorably for you.

Note: **PLEASE**, no groveling, smarmy, cringe-inducing *"I hope that college will turn me into the [insert brown-nosing here] I know I can be."* Fawning and "sucking up" are easily recognized and sternly frowned upon.

If you've done your research on the college to which you are applying, you'll know what will or won't work for this specific institution, and can write your essay in a way that'll show the Board you would make a good fit. The following Case Study reflects one student's experience with having to write an applications essay for a super selective private school.

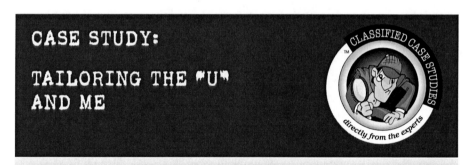

CASE STUDY:

TAILORING THE "U" AND ME

Part of the application process for undergraduate admission to many universities is the submission of an application letter of intent. I've always understood that this process helps you to differentiate yourself from others in the large applicant pool. I attended a small private liberal arts school in Austin, Texas. St. Edward's University required an application letter, which at first made me feel nervous, but after discussing the subject with my parents and some of my favorite teachers, I knew exactly what I needed to write. My academic record was going to speak for itself, but it was up to me to show the admissions committee who I was and what I was going to add to the student body at St. Edward's.

St. Edward's is a Catholic institution, so it probably didn't hurt that I'd attended Catholic school most of my life and could play up my desire to attend an institution that had a vested interest in my "moral" development. I also focused on all of the extra-curricular activities I'd been involved in like sports and volunteering, and touched on what I wanted to achieve during my college experience. I discussed the value my parents had always placed on education and how both my grandfather and my mother were educators-turned-principals.

I am sure I dropped in a quote from Walt Whitman or some other transcendental poet who valued individualism, the real zeitgeist of America, and all its other dreams and promises of success. All in all, I figured it was just one more hoop that I had to jump through, but if I could pull it off it would help my chances of getting into a great private school. (At the very least, it would show the admissions people that I could write in complete sentences, conjugate verbs, and even properly use a semicolon.)

Thanks in part to my solid writing skills and education, both at St. Edwards in Austin and Xavier University in Cincinnati, I am now working for a grant-funded project and will be performing a lot of administrative coordination work, along with editing, writing, communication, and marketing and public-relations material.

— Christina Burke-Tillema, M.A.

As you can see in this Case Study, the author was able to use strong, true aspects of her life that she knew would be considered to be of importance to the college of her choice and would help her cause — without fawning and "sucking up." She crafted a powerful essay centered around those concepts, and in the end wound up receiving admission to St. Edward's.

CHAPTER 8

How Do You Prepare to Write This Thing?

Depending on your creative abilities and strengths, you might view the writing process as an evil monster lurking under the bed — or the cozy blankey on top into which you can snuggle and let your imagination flow. For many students, writing is the most difficult part of school, while others look forward to the chance to show their ability and be creative.

Bear in mind that the monster lurking under the bed isn't as scary as it seems (because he doesn't really exist), and that once you force yourself to face it, you'll realize that you have wasted a lot of time worrying. Yes, you *do* need to write your application essays, but the longer you let your fears build up, the more terrifying the process will become.

We've already talked about attention-grabbing and hooks. For the time being, let's concentrate on the most important issue at hand: *How do you start to write this thing?*

Avoid Procrastination!

The advice you heard in previous chapters is back! Some of us are born, raised, continue to be, and will die, procrastinators — *procrastinators unite! . . . tomorrow.* You may possess a strong tendency to put things off until the very last minute. You may stall and stall until there is no time left at all. As a result, your focus — and your time — may be limited.

Listen very carefully: **do not procrastinate on the college admissions essay!** If your application is due on February 1st, don't wait until January 31st to begin writing the essay. You need sufficient time to complete the essay to the best of your abilities. If you wait until the last minute, your essay could appear creatively weak to the admissions committee who might deny admission just like that that. You can avoid this with proper time, effort, and motivation.

Prepare Yourself — Don't Expect to Just Sit Down and Start Writing

A grocery list, yes; a quick e-mail to your best friend, sure — but anything that requires serious concentration and has a real purpose can't be spat out as soon as you sit down. Long before you take keyboard or pen in hand, you should be thinking and strategizing. You might do well to keep a small notebook (more about that in a moment) on hand throughout your day for those occasional *aha!* thoughts — those unexpected flashes of inspiration as you ride the bus or mow the yard. It's not reasonable to expect yourself to just sit right down, cold turkey, and expect to produce a good essay.

Helpful tip: Take notes everywhere! Whether you keep notes and lists electronically, or use a pencil to write in a 50-cent pocket notebook, have something on hand at all times. When a random thought comes to your mind, you don't want to forget it before you get it written down. The notes don't have to be neat or legible to anyone except yourself.

Set Beginning and Ending Dates and Stick with Them

When writing, it's helpful to have a definite target start-date set — one that allows you plenty of time to meet your deadline — and to hold firm to it. Unless there's an emergency, consider yourself unavailable during your writing time.

So, what exactly qualifies as an *emergency*? An illness or accident requiring unexpected surgery for you or an immediate family member, your house burns down, a tornado is tearing down the street, or the four horsemen of the apocalypse have appeared on your doorstep for tea.

What is *not* an emergency? A last-minute invitation to Becky's party, a chance to go on a boat ride, a co-worker wanting to change shifts (for non-emergency reasons — see prior sentences), your headphones broke, you stayed out too late last night, the weather's excellent for shooting hoops, your best friend Eric just got a new car, Jenny's cat just had kittens, you'd rather nap . . . you get the idea.

The bottom line is that parties and boats rides and basketball and kittens will come and go, but college work will require discipline, and this is as good a time to start as any. Tell your friends, family, and co-workers that you will be unavailable during your writing times. Most people understand how important this is and won't interfere with the time . . . but, as an added precaution, you may want to turn off your cell phone and avoid getting online while beginning your work — just avoid the temptation altogether.

Under license from Shutterstock.com

To Outline (or Not to Outline)? . . . That is the Question

People have different opinions on outlines. Some can't write without them, while some think they hold back your writing's potential. Here are three ways you can approach outlining your college admissions essay:

1) *No Outline*

   Some people can have an idea and just let it roll onto the page. They are able to keep their thoughts organized well enough without first charting their plan in an outline, and the writing still has structure and is cohesive.

2) *Outline First*

   Many writers plan out the entire piece before they begin. Laying out the introduction and thesis, main body with supporting points, and conclusion, and filling in with details and anecdotes to make the writing sparkle, can help keep these folks on the right track.

3) *Outline Later*

Some people use a combination of these two approaches. They get their thoughts down on paper, and *then* create an outline from their draft. These writers can see the main topics appearing in their first attempt, and, after viewing the first piece as a whole, are able to move or change parts of the writing as needed with the help of an outline.

> ➤ **Here's another tip:** Once you begin your draft-writing, don't change topics unless there is a very good reason to do so. By now, you will have spent at least a couple of weeks (if not more) thinking, taking notes, and preparing. You have ideas taking form in your mind, and it is counterproductive to suddenly decide that another topic might be better. You would be, in essence, starting from scratch, and all the weeks of planning for the other topic will have been eaten up! Time has a way of passing awfully quickly when a deadline is coming up and starting over will only slow you down.

DON'T PLAGIARIAZE!

There is a naughty p-word you have heard many times before: *plagiarism.* **DO NOT DO IT.** Remember that if you use someone else's work (and in a personal essay such as for college admissions, that should be rare if at all), you **must** put quotation marks around the borrowed words and give appropriate credit wherever it is required, whether in a footnote, endnote, or on a Works Cited page. If you do so and stay within the boundaries of reasonable borrowing, you won't be plagiarizing.

However, at this stage of college writing, you may not want to borrow at all. Citations can get messy. It's easier (not to mention quicker) to just stick to your own words. There will plenty of time for academic writing in the next two to four years.

We've discussed how modern technology has, paradoxically, both helped and hindered current higher education. Perhaps better than any other, plagiarism is a great example of this. Although students have countless essays, articles, and the like available thanks to the internet, teachers, administrators, and Admission Board members have the same — and many more — resources, as well. Did you know there are sites dedicated exclusively to helping educators ferret out suspected acts of plagiarism? And even without the sophisticated technology, the Admissions Board can just as easily Google that same sentence or paragraph you did to copy into your essay. It is their job to find out if you've plagiarized — and they're good at it.

Remember that plagiarizing shows a lack of creativity, and pure laziness. The chance of not getting caught is not worth the price you may end up paying if you are. Although your admissions essay may not be an "award-winner," if you plagiarize, it can be the thing that ends your college dreams, and for reasons far more severe than simply being "boring" or "typical."

CHAPTER 9

Food For Thought When Writing Your Essay

Y ou've got this. If you have at least a basic set of writing skills, with a ton of thought and a little bit of creativity, you should be able to develop and write an essay that'll impress the admissions committee. They're not only looking at your writing skills, but also making an effort to understand you as a person. Colleges and universities are of course interested in your academic strengths and weaknesses, but there is increasing pressure on you to demonstrate your own character and personality. Your application essay gives you a chance to shine!

Here are some basic things to consider before writing.

Be Prepared for a Variety of Questions and Essay Topics

Chapter 7 talked about how different colleges have different requirements regarding the application essays. Some questions may be incredibly basic and require some third-person observation on your part: *If you were a newcomer, how would you describe your hometown?* Some questions might be more introspective: *Please describe your strengths and weaknesses in better detail,* or *Name the person who has provided the most influence in your life to date. What has this individual taught you about dedication and perseverance?* Still other questions may seem totally random: *You are delivering pizza to a new home in an upscale neighborhood, and the customers (male and female) answer the door in the nude. What do you do?* Or *If you could be any famous animal in history, which one would it be, and why?*

Along with knowing what your college of choice considers to be priority, remember that one of your duties as an applicant is to find out the nature of the questions that you can expect from each institution and prepare yourself. If you're applying to a variety of schools, you might be required to answer the same kinds of questions more than once, even if they are worded differently from one application to the next. You may need to tweak an essay to make it fit with the exact wording of the question: College A: *If you could be any famous animal in history, which would it be, and why?* is very closely related to: College B: *You have a choice to be Robert E. Lee's horse, Traveler, or Roy Rogers's horse, Trigger. Which would you be, and why?*

College A's question doesn't limit your choice of animal to be a horse, and lets you use your imagination, expanding to lions, tigers, and bears, etc. College B's question not only narrows the field to horses, but further limits it to only two specific horses, leaving virtually no wiggle-room for spontaneous creativity.

For example, someone applying to College A might write that he would like to have been the Trojan Horse (especially if he is applying to University of Southern California (USC), who are known as The Trojans), but if an applicant were to send the same essay to College B (University of California, Los Angeles (UCLA), the cross-town rival of USC), even the most well-written Trojan Horse answer would suggest to the admissions officer that this student is not truly paying attention or, worse, too lazy to write a second essay.

Make no mistake; Admissions Boards are aware of the questions asked by other college admissions offices, particularly of nearby schools. They tend to receive applications from many of the same students, so don't be surprised if an admissions officer easily sees through your scheme.

Now, what you realistically *could* do in this situation is write to College B's question in such a way as it also answers College A: *Of all famous animals in history, I would most like to be Traveler because even though he was on the side of the losing Confederacy, he never let his master down and was there from Bull Run to Appomattox. Or, I would like to be Trigger, because when he died, Roy had him stuffed in a taxidermist and put on display in a museum, so he truly "lived on," in a manner of speaking.* While this is a more honest approach, you must make sure that a multi-school reply meets each school's particular criteria.

> Valerie Lasko, whose Case Study is shown in Chapter 5 and who introduced the applications essay for us, confirms the less-arduous theory: "As I recall, I tried to use the same essay for each college application, but changed/tweaked it some based on each college's question." As her case reveals, she was accepted into all five colleges to which she applied. She obviously did a good job of writing and, later on, tweaking, according to the individual institutions' questions.

Humor

The more creative of applicants may be tempted to have some fun with these questions, particularly those that seem ridiculous, but this is not the time to strut your comedic stuff. Take this part of the application process seriously, to help improve your position as a prospective applicant. What *would* you do if someone answered the door naked? Act professionally, hand over the pizza box, and politely look away while waiting for payment? Burst out laughing and point at their nudity? Start removing your own clothes to ease the tension? Scurry away screaming in abject horror and embarrassment?

Your college acceptance may depend on a thoughtful and introspective essay to promote a strong case for your admission. There will be time for literary mischief later on in your college career; save it for then. Some writing courses will actually encourage a bit of humorous writing, and perhaps the campus newspaper has a column space for you — but let's first get you into the school.

Here's another Case Study written by a young woman currently working on her Doctorate — and who (as you will see), has never felt truly comfortable with writing.

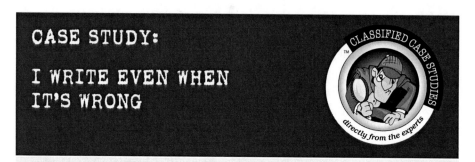

CASE STUDY:

I WRITE EVEN WHEN IT'S WRONG

I think this has to be one of the more difficult pieces of writing I have had to do — writing about writing. It is akin to discussing the importance of breathing or blood circulating throughout the veins. How much time can you spend talking about why you must breathe or why blood must move around throughout the body? The necessity of those two functions should be so obvious that a prolonged discussion on the matter is pointless.

I am writing my PhD thesis in Economics while also working as a full-time college instructor in the subject. To get to this point, I've written my way through high school, college, and graduate school in English classes, on exams, for scientific papers, and comprehensive exams. I've been taught how to write more effectively, I've learned by doing, and I've adjusted my own writing style to avoid what I dislike reading in other works.

I cannot survive in my profession without writing. On the one hand, I need to write for professional publication, which requires one tone or style. On the other hand, I have to write as a teacher, which requires a completely different approach. Most students are unfamiliar with Economics, and the language of the discipline turns many of them away before they can get comfortable with the field. I've found that reworking the more sophisticated writing into more everyday language smooths this transition and allows me to later use the formal terminology with a greater degree of success.

However, to put it mildly, writing is not my favorite activity. The hardest part is putting into words what I want to say. I usually have a general outline of the topic at hand, but I'll start to write a sentence, delete it, rewrite, and repeat. Rarely do the thoughts and words flow seamlessly. I have to work hard for every paragraph. These difficulties aren't as pressing when I am writing for lectures, but they are exacerbated in non-academic writing. This is true even when I am writing in a diary! I've never seriously attempted fictional writing because story ideas or characters just won't pop into my head.

Overall, I write best when I am passionate about something, but even then the aforementioned issues still rear their heads in the process. I love the *idea* of writing, just as I've always loved the idea of running or skating. The latter two I can practice to get better, but I think that the difficulties I have in the writing process are simply a part me, and will always be there. However, I am usually quite happy with the finished product, which is what really counts!

— Katharine (Katie) Kontak, Economics Instructor
Bowling Green (OH) State University

The "admissions essay" Ms. Kontak wrote would be considered interesting, insightful, and reveals the potential student's personality and abilities. She begins with an interesting conundrum, winds through the body of the essay detailing what and how she has had to write so far, admits to her shortcomings, and ends on a positive note. She doesn't try to over-flatter or overstate her desire to do what this hypothetical school will no doubt require (write, write, and write some more), but her approach, on the whole, shows her determination to work hard, do her best, and achieve.

Remember: even though writing may be a challenge for you, many who share your same discomfort have found their way through, and have even — by golly! — *improved* as they pursued their courses.

Your Environment for Writing

Where do you think you would be most comfortable writing? Is the old familiar desk in your room the best spot for you, or should the laptop or notepad occasionally be carried somewhere different, just for a change of scenery that might better inspire you?

If you've decided to try going somewhere totally different than your normal writing spot, be sure to check it out first. Can you sit comfortably enough, and a find a suitable position in which to type or write by hand? Is there enough light? If you're outside, are there restroom facilities (besides the nearest tree or bush, of course) nearby? Is there shelter, in case the weather turns? Is it the season for annoying insects or freezing rain? Will there be a ton of other people around crowding you and causing unwanted noise? Any or all of these factors could distract you and keep you from creating your best work. For the sake of convenience, you may be better off just staying put in your customary work area, but there is something to be said, especially when you need a burst of creativity, for elsewhere, even just for the start of your project.

Under license from Shutterstock.com

Maybe you like music playing as you work; others prefer silence. Some students like to have the TV on, just for the comforting background noise. One strategy doesn't work for everybody; there is no right or wrong way to work. The important thing is to get your essay started, but beyond that, it's up to you to determine your own appropriate writing atmosphere.

Get Your Materials Ready

Make sure your materials are prepared and well-stocked. We've been talking about issues that will continue to be important even after you have been accepted and begun your college career, and this is no exception. Whether it be when you write your undergraduate admissions essay or your dissertation, have your tools gathered and in place *before* you begin writing. Try to avoid having those moments of unnecessary interruption when you re-alize you've forgotten a pencil or your laptop charger in the other room.

"Be prepared" might be the Boy Scouts' motto, but it is also the college student's (or college applicant's) salvation. Being prepared by knowing *what* is expected and *when* it is expected, having prepared notes and out-lines, knowing where you will be most comfortable and likely to find your best creativity, and having all of your materials at the ready will all help assure the success of your application essay and many more writing assign-ments to come. Unlike procrastination and plagiarism, this is the *good* p-word: preparation!

Before actually talking about the act of writing itself, and in case you are still floundering about for a thesis statement, Chapter 10 is devoted to helping you stir up some possible ideas for your essay. These are not meant to be your actual thesis statement, but they may jump-start your mind to-ward a direction that might not have otherwise occurred to you. If you al-ready have a good, strong topic in mind, you can skip to Chapter 11.

Some Possible Essay Thought Starters

Again, please note that most of these are not meant to be thesis statements, or the whole point of your essay. They are merely for writing practice and to perhaps help you get those writing juices flowing.

Categories

Animals

Do you have pets or have you spent much time around animals?

Have you ever had a favorite pet?

What have you learned from animals?

Do you have any career interests that involve animals?

What is your favorite zoo or circus creature?

Athletics

Do you participate in athletics?

What is your favorite sport, either to do or watch?

Have you ever suffered a serious injury while participating in an athletic activity? If so, how has that impacted your life?

Do you feel that today's "trash-talking" and "in-your-face" type of play is poor sportsmanship or just healthy competition?

Are there any athletes you really admire or dislike? Why?

Do you think that professional athletes are setting good examples or should work harder to set better examples for kids?

How do you feel about athletes who are arrested, caught cheating in the game, or doing something else that is illegal like steroid use or gambling? Should they be banned from their sport, and how many chances do you think they should they be given?

Careers

If you had a "dream job," what would it be?

What would be your idea of a "nightmare job?"

What do you see as the biggest challenge facing someone trying to break into the workforce for the first time?

Do you think you would make a good supervisor/foreperson/manager? Why or why not?

What was your first job? What was the most important thing you learned from it?

How do you envision your retirement?

Community

To what sort of community do you feel you belong?

Do you participate in any community projects?

What do you most like or dislike about your community, and why?

If you were in charge of your community, what would you do to change it for the better?

Current Events

Do you keep yourself up to date on what is going on in your community, the country, and the world? With which form of media do you do this? TV, radio, newspaper, internet news sources?

Within your lifetime, what do you think has been the most global significant issue — global warming, failing world economies, war and poverty, etc.?

Is there a topic that you think is overpublicized and the importance over exaggerated in the media?

Dreams

What are some of your recurring dreams? What are the common themes?

What have been some of your most memorable dreams?

Do you think dreams hold any special meaning and can be interpreted?

Can dreams foretell the future?

Have you ever been able to solve a problem in your dreams that you were not able to solve while awake?

Entertainment

What is your favorite TV show, and why?

Which do you enjoy more: going out to the movies, or staying home and watching a movie on the couch?

Do you enjoy live concerts? What about the symphony, opera, or ballet?

If you could become any famous TV or cinema personality, who would you be and why?

Do you enjoy watching older shows that originally aired before you were born? Why or why not?

Families

How would you describe your immediate family (like your mom, dad, and siblings)?

How would you describe your extended family?

If you are an only child, have you ever wished you had siblings? If you have siblings, have you ever wished you were an only child?

Of all of your relatives, living or dead, who do you think has had the most positive influence on you, and why?

Which of your ancestors would you most like to meet?

If you choose to have children later on in life, what do you think will be your biggest challenge as a parent?

High School

What has been your fondest memory of high school?

What has been your biggest challenge thus far and how did you overcome it?

Which teachers are you most likely remember long after graduation?

When was your most embarrassing moment?

What extracurricular activities have you participated in and enjoyed?

What do you think accounts for the current disturbing trend of violence in high schools? How can we solve the problem?

Historical Events

What, in your opinion, has been the most significant historical event to happen during your lifetime? How has it affected you?

If you were to become a famous historical figure, how would you feel about the way you've been memorialized by modern society?

Do you believe that spirits haunt historic places like Gettysburg, Pennsylvania or Savannah, Georgia?

What historical event or time period interests you most?

You've gone back in time and are on a famous, historical ship. Which would it be, and why? If you knew from history class that the ship would sink, would you try to prevent it from doing so? How?

Hobbies

What is your favorite pastime? How did you first get involved in this activity?

Do you share this hobby with others?

Do you feel the hobby could eventually become financially lucrative?

Has your interest in one hobby led to others?

About how much of your spending money goes toward your hobby?

Lifestyle

How important is material wealth to you?

What is your favorite automobile, and why? Are you more of a compact, pick-up, SUV, or sports car type?

If you could own any kind of residence, what would it be? A house, mansion, tree-house, RV?

You have a date and unlimited spending money. What do you do?

You have a date with the same person, but are now completely broke. What do you do?

Do you find it comical or disturbing to see the extent to which some people will go to hide their age or change their appearance?

You are given the choice to keep only one of your more expensive forms of entertainment — will you keep your computer, cell phone, X-Box, etc.?

Do you find it interesting to keep up with the social lives, legal problems, marriages and divorces, and little details of the lives of celebrities? Or do you find it vapid and insensitive?

What do you think of reality shows?

You are getting married and are ecstatic about it. Is it important to have a fancy, expensive wedding or would you prefer a more intimate ceremony?

Music

What is your favorite kind of music, and why?

Is there any particular song or musical composition that has special significance to you?

If you could play any musical instrument, which would it be?

What is the first song you can ever recall hearing?

Do you enjoy singing alone or in a group?

Has a particular lyric ever moved you to tears?

Nature

What is your favorite or least favorite season?

What force of nature do you find most fascinating or frightening?

Would you rather lounge on the beach or go camping in a forest?

What is your favorite kind of body of water, and why?

Have you ever seen an especially beautiful sunrise, sunset, or snowfall? Describe it and how it made you feel.

What you think when you see the moon and stars?

Do you like to find shapes in the clouds?

Does the average thunderstorm frighten you?

Religion/ Spirituality

Do you believe in a Higher Power?

Do you think that religion can be harmful?

Have you ever had what you consider to be an epiphany or a moment of spiritual truth that changed the course of your life?

Do you believe in life after death?

Do you believe in spirits, ghosts, or poltergeists?

Do you lend any credence to spiritualists, mediums, or parapsychologists?

Do you think there is any truth to the near-death experiences, where people declared clinically dead have been revived and tell of seeing a white light or some other occurrence?

Social Issues

What do you think is this country's most pressing social issue, and how should it be addressed?

Do you think the United States has overstepped in helping social issues in other countries? Do you think more should be done?

Have you ever felt especially upset by hearing of someone being mistreated, socially abused, or neglected?

Is it possible to overcome prejudices and stereotypical point of views, or is this an unavoidable part of human nature?

Travel

Where would you most travel in the United States? Elsewhere?

What is your favorite way of traveling?

Are you afraid to fly?

Have you ever traveled anywhere? What's your favorite memory of the experience?

You are going on a cruise: do you choose to go to the Caribbean, Alaska, or Europe?

If you could live in any foreign country, which would it be?

Do you think you would ever enjoy doing out-of-country service work, like with the Peace Corps or a church group?

You have an opportunity to go to Niagara Falls for the first time. You may choose to go either in the winter when the crowds are gone but many of the attractions are closed, or in the summer where you'll face long lines but be able to experience everything Niagara has to offer. Which do you choose?

Scenarios

Think of how you would respond to these situations:

- You are walking down a city street, and see someone running your way, being chased by a police officer. What do you do, and why?

- You are driving alone on a country road late at night, and accidentally strike a dog who has wandered into the road. The dog is obviously hurt, but is not dead. What do you do?

- You are in a restaurant, and see money fall out of a man's pocket as he starts to leave. You cannot see the denominations, but there are obviously more than a few bills lying on the floor. Do you let him know, or is it "finders-keepers?"

- While at work, your boss compliments you on a report that you did not do. The coworker who actually wrote it is a real slacker and not someone you get along with. How do you respond to your boss?

- A longtime friend has deeply hurt your feelings; you are upset and incredibly angry. How do you react?

- You go to someone's house to do a small handyman repair around lunchtime. As a thank you, he brings you a plate with some food that you are not allergic to, but just do not like. What do you do?

- You are in a fender-bender which is the other (extremely apologetic) driver's fault. Your car is not severely damaged and your insurance company assures you that the repairs will be covered. However, though neither of you were injured in the accident, an attorney calls the next day and tells you that there are grounds for a lawsuit against the driver at fault and that you could receive a large settlement. What do you do?

- You have found a cat and taken him in. He is affectionate, friendly, well-behaved, and fits into your household as if he had been a part of your family forever. A month later, you see a "Missing Cat" poster, complete with a photo of the exact cat you've taken in. Do you contact the owners?

- While sitting in class before the bell rings, you overhear two students behind you whispering about they're going to cheat on the exam. Do you let the teacher know?

- You are painting the outside of your neighbor's house for some extra cash, but you fall two stories off the ladder and seriously injure yourself. It is nobody's fault, but the law says you can sue the homeowners because the accident occurred on their property. Do you?

- You snuck out of your house and are at a party across town with your best friend. He is far too drunk to drive; you're sober, but your learner's permit doesn't allow you to drive with anyone other than family members at night. No one at the party will help you get him home. You have no money for a cab and the buses out of service. What do you do?

- You are a clerk at a small, independently-owned hamburger stand in a rough neighborhood. A man comes in and demands you empty the cash register. He does not appear to be armed, but the store owner, whom you like and who has been good to you, keeps a handgun under the counter. What do you do?

- You accidentally take home a teammate's gym bag, which you've mistaken for your own. Upon opening it, you discover packets that you realize contain an illegal drug. How do you handle this?

- A 16-year-old long-time friend has secretly run away from home. With your reluctant permission, she has told her mother she is spending the night with you when she is really leaving town. The mother calls and asks to speak to her later that evening, so you panic and say "She is in the shower," and the mother takes your word for it. After hanging up, you are extremely guilt-stricken. Do you call the mother back and confess, explaining the scheme, or let it go and trust your friend to know what is best for herself?

- Your tuition to your dream school will amount to just under $40,000. You have found out you are compatible with a wealthy older cousin who desperately needs a kidney transplant. They offer you the $40,000 for your kidney — do you take advantage of the offer?

- You find a wallet filled with money, but no credit cards or ID, in an area with no security cameras. You realize that it will be almost impossible to track down the owner of the wallet and money. What do you do?

- You witness a car accident, and it looks as if there might be injuries. You are already running late for the third time this week, and your boss has said that she will fire you if you are late again — no excuses! The job pays well and will help pay for your college tuition. What do you do?

- You are walking through a public park, and see an elderly woman sitting alone on a bench, looking lost and ready to cry. What do you do? Would your response change if the sad person was a young man?

- In a grocery store, you see a young mother spank her misbehaving toddler on the rear end with her open palm. She only spanks her child once, but another woman begins to scold her quite harshly. What is your reaction?

Here's another real heads-up when it comes to college curriculum: even if the question doesn't end in *why?*, as you might see in some of the listed ideas above mainly because it gets so repetitive, you must *always* assume (unless told otherwise) that a mere *yes* or *no* is not going to suffice. Just for example, take a look at one of the scenarios again: *Yes*, or even the high school-enforced complete sentence, *Yes, I call the owners of the cat* is not sufficient. The *why*, the reasons behind your answers are more important than the answers themselves.

A good percentage of the above scenarios are things that many people have probably experienced in some form, and some of them occur to students by high school. What this should tell you is that, as we've said before, please don't think there's nothing in your life worth talking about in your application essay. And really, your responses will give your audience a fairly good idea of the kind of person you are and what you consider important, either ethically or morally, in life.

CHAPTER 11

Ready, Set, WRITE! (Phase 1)

The day is finally here: the day you've marked down as the day you'll begin writing your application essay. This is the day that will help change the course of your life; the day you have both dreaded and anticipated because books like this one make it sound like such a big deal!

For at least several weeks now, you've been seriously thinking about what you'll be doing today, making notes, reading other students' successful essays, deciding where the best place would be to set up shop, and you have reminded your friends that you are off-limits during your writing hours. Just to make sure, you have turned off your cell phone and have resisted the urge to constantly get online. You have all the necessary materials gathered — your notes, dictionary and thesaurus, chargers and power cords, and enough paper and ink in case you decide you need or want to print something. You are finally ready.

Keep this in mind: any of the writing "tips" we've already shared or will share are only suggestions. Remember our discussion about outline vs. no outline — what does or does not work for one person may or may not work for you. You can strip our advice down to what you most need to remember; you know yourself better than anyone else.

Lower Your Expectations

One of the most serious roadblocks to writing is that feeling of having to produce something of the magnitude of, let's say J.K. Rowling. You are no Rowling, nor are you Harry Potter; there is no magic spell that will make you the world's greatest essayist.

Because this essay seems so important, it's only natural that you feel pressured to produce your absolute best work ever. But sometimes, this expectation to create greatness is one that J.K. Rowling herself might fail to live up to.

On the other hand, your goal should always be to do your absolute best. Push yourself to create an essay that shows how committed you are to succeeding in college, and that you're willing to work hard to obtain that success. Be honest in your writing and work hard — that's all you should expect of yourself.

Take Breaks

Another suggestion that may surprise you to stop once you have gained some momentum. That's right — you heard us! That being said, momentum doesn't mean having written two consecutive sentences. It means when you've made enough progress that you feel confident in the form your essay has begun to take on. If your writing begins to flow, let it flow! Take breaks when you feel your writing juices running dry. Find a good stopping place from which you can easily begin writing again, and step away for a bit.

Don't work on and on until you hit a wall. Take a break before this happens to recharge so those walls are avoided altogether!

Let's use the following scenarios to explain the reasoning behind this strategy:

Most of you, at some time or other, have worked on projects — whether they be school assignments or something you enjoy doing as a hobby. In almost any project, you might find a time when you run into a snag, or some sort of problem that you just can't seem to solve at the moment.

Let's assume you've worked on an essay for five hours straight. It was going great until you developed writer's block. Now that you've stepped away at this point, how much do you dread having to go back to that project, knowing what you are up against?

On the other hand, say you took a break two hours in when a good stopping place presented itself. How do you feel about returning to that project, when everything is coming along smoothly and you can pick right up where you left off? You can think about it while you're on your break and actually look forward to getting back to writing, rather than worrying about whether your writer's block will return when you sit back down.

Someday in your future job, you will find your weekends (or whatever time off you get) are much more enjoyable if you leave work on Friday with projects at a good stopping point to be picked back up on Monday. Many a weekend has been hampered by the dread of what is waiting for you on Monday.

This can also be true of writing, especially if you are one who has been struggling with the thought of this essay. If you find that you've been moving along well in your writing for a while, try to find a good stopping point for a quick break, so that you can come back to the essay ready to pick up and take back off.

Think about it this way: how do you feel all day knowing that you are going out for your favorite pizza for dinner? You anticipate and savor. On the other hand, leaving on a bad note can be like knowing you have a root-canal dentist appointment immediately after school or work, and dreading it so much you can't enjoy your day at all.

 ## When should I stop?

- If you've been working a long time and have gained some good momentum, but know there is no way you'll be able to make it all the way to the end of your essay today, find a good place and stop.

- If you even *begin* to suspect that you are coming to a real speed bump, stop before that bump grows into a concrete wall. You'll probably find the solution much more easily if you let it marinate in your mind overnight.

- If you did think you could make it to the end, but find yourself struggling down the homestretch, finish the sentence or paragraph you're on and stop. This is a classic indication that you are just tired. If you're just winding down the paper, you'll be able to pick right back up next time with little or no problem.

- If you make it all the way through that first draft, stop there. Give yourself not only a pat on the back, but also a good 24 hours before you return to the essay. *Don't* begin to proofread or re-write right away.

Use Highlights

If there's a word or phrase that isn't working for you but you can't figure out how to rephrase it, highlight it. You can come back to it later, during the revision stage. Right now, your focus should be on getting as many words written or typed as you can while you're creativity is still flowing. Refine later!

Under license from Shutterstock.com

Save, Save, Save Your Work!

You've probably heard the advice to always, *always* save your work. Save, save, save your work, and save, save, save to a backup — usually a USB-port flash-drive. Don't forget to remove the storage device from your computer when you are finished; if there is an unexpected power surge, the device can be fried or otherwise ruined right along with your CPU. But nevertheless, saving your work as you go can prevent a spontaneous loss of all your time and energy. You wouldn't want to start all over!

Finding the Right Words

Don't waste time with the occasional speed-bump of trying to find the perfect word. This is one of those bumps that can become a huge barrier if you let it; but it doesn't need to be. There are several ways to keep your momentum going: type in the "almost-but-not-quite-right" word and highlight it. In a later stage of the essay's development, you can always thumb through the thesaurus if you still haven't found the right word.

Similarly, if you type in a word but the spelling in reality looks strange, the dictionary (not autocorrect — more about that later) can wait. This is another case where a highlighter will be your friend.

Helpful tip: set up a separate file into which you can dump some of your writing that may seem "not quite right" and yet, too good to just delete altogether. There may be a paragraph or sentence that sounds solid, but just doesn't belong where you are right now. If you hit a wall, you can turn to this file for ideas you had earlier or even whole paragraphs which might now have a home in your essay. For instance, you might be working on your introduction and suddenly think of an absolutely perfect way to end the essay. Rather than do the lazy thing and just hit ENTER a few times, you would be better off putting that ending in an extra file. By the time you finish your essay, you might not remember that the line is still there, hanging out at the bottom of your document, out of sight, or that you even wrote it at all.

When You're Ready to Stop

Finally, when you do decide to stop for the day, wherever you are in the process, try to leave yourself "briefed" as to where you intend to pick up — your next idea and where you hope to go with it. Don't make the mistake of thinking *Oh, sure, I'll remember what I'm going to say next* — it's way too easy to lose the train of thought once you have a good night's sleep. Make notes to yourself on a separate piece of paper or type them into your document using a different color font at your stopping point, and close up shop for now.

You've done well today, and you're finally starting to see some results for all the hard preparation (and worrying) you have been doing these past few weeks. Relax and enjoy your evening; turn your cell phone back on, go see Jenny's new kittens, and know that you have gotten past the hardest part of writing your applications essay: starting.

CHAPTER 12

Ready, Set, WRITE! (Phase 2)

Congratulations! You've made a good start on your applications essay. There's still a long way to go, but it will be much easier this time around because you've taken the all-important and terrifying leap by starting.

Whether you actually made it all the way through the first draft or have only partly completed it, there is an additional bonus to having come this far: while you were playing with the kittens or riding in Eric's new car after that first effort, your mind was subconsciously working. Like a cow chewing its cud, your creative subconscious loves to ruminate on projects like this. Your subconscious has been "chewing" on what you have accomplished thus far, and what you hope to accomplish at your next sitting, which will be either completing or revising your first draft. You may or may not have actively let yourself think about the task, but in truth, there was thinking being done — and plenty of it.

Rereading

When you return to work, whether you are revising or completing your first draft, read through what you have already written. At this point, don't waste time on your highlights or notes you made while drafting. Some of us want to have everything *just right* before we continue, but this is one of those times that it is best to ignore the *make-it-just-right* compulsion and move on.

Under license from Shutterstock.com

Right now, you're just rereading to reintroduce yourself to your essay, so that you can go forward with it from the point at which you left off. You might see some minor glitches, spelling, punctuation, and such, but leave them be and don't get distracted by them; that's what the revision stage is for.

A visual: Picture, again, that stone carver from before. Let's say he is working on a statue. On day one, he roughs out the statue's head, torso, and arms before leaving for the night. The next morning, he comes in and sees all the flaws, rough spots, and whatever else bothers him about the head, torso, and arms, and rather than continuing on with the legs and feet, he begins to re-work the first part. Two things unquestionably happen: 1) he risks losing the sense of proportion to the overall statue and 2) he ends up too tired to work any further. Even worse, a third and fourth crises might also occur: he could raise more flaws that will have to be fixed, and — worst case scenario — might end up ruining the original work and have to start all over again because he's jumped around and lost sight of where in the project he was before he started *fixing*.

If you haven't finished the first draft, do your best to finish it now, in this sitting. This is particularly important if you will not have a chance to do anything of significance on it for another few days for some reason. One of the biggest issues teachers and professors see when reading students' papers is a lack of continuity, both in thought and style. It's easy to tell when an assignment had been shelved too often by the changes in tone and style. Even good, solid professional writers can have trouble maintaining continuity — hence the stereotype of creative people adamantly demanding solitude and uninterrupted work time. Your essay will be more cohesive if you can keep those first-draft sessions to a minimum.

Revising

You may love your first draft and be itching to send it off to the admissions officers right away. Before you do, you'd still be wise to take some time to revise your essay. Everyone, students and professionals alike, can benefit from a good revision. Now is the time to go back and fix those little things you noticed in your re-reading. If you made any highlights (word-choices, spellings, a phrase that needs further work, etc.) that can be fixed easily, go back to these now.

Don't Rely on Spell-Check!

Spell-Check and autocorrect are valuable tools, but are not a cure-all; at best, they can lull you into a false sense of security about the "correctness" of your writing. As you've noticed, the English language has many homonyms that Spell-Check and autocorrect might not catch.

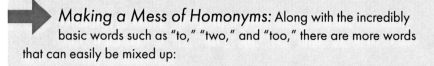

Making a Mess of Homonyms: Along with the incredibly basic words such as "to," "two," and "too," there are more words that can easily be mixed up:

- *She road down the rode on her horse.*

- *The principle's first principal for his students was honesty.*

- *Weather it rains or snows, the whether cannot hold us up.*

- *In a vein attempt to stop the bleeding, she covered her vain.*

(In case you have not figured it out, those homonyms have been deliberately switched.) Spell-Check would not have caught any of those errors; it is up to you to ensure you use the correct spelling or word-form accordingly.

Along with Spell-Check's little red, squiggly line, there is another computer-assist aide called Grammar Check which is usually shown by a blue line. This can help catch some errors — mainly punctuation, or if the sentence does not make sense as written — but again, it's not fool-proof. A classic example of a sentence that might be totally incorrect, but devoid of any red or green squiggle-lines would be something like this: *Tom said he was defiantly going to talk to his father about going to Auburn University.* Did Tom intend to show "attitude" with his father (a University of Georgia alumnus), or was the sentence supposed to say that Tom would *definitely* talk about attending Auburn? Obviously, Spell/Grammar-Check would give this sentence a clean bill of non-squiggled health, but unless Tom and his father are truly at odds, this is incorrect.

Bear in mind, computers are only as smart as the human being who is controlling their keyboards and reading the screen, so try to avoid such mistakes, and especially avoid over-relying on these "checking" functions.

Two far better tools to use when you're really stuck on spelling or word choice are a dictionary and a thesaurus. Whether you use hard copies or ones you found on the internet, you'll be glad you did.

Proofreading

Proofreading is a more exact form of revision. During this stage, you will make sure every single word is spelled correctly, double check every punctuation mark, and not rest until the entire piece is technically perfect — or as close as it can be. This may sound daunting, but here are some tips to help make the process work smoothly.

Under license from Shutterstock.com

Recruit other eyes!

Of course, you will proofread your own work carefully several times before "this thing can be put to bed" (that is journalism-speak for "finished"), but you must, must, *must* also ask someone else to proofread, as well. Relying on only your own proofing is about as "iffy" as relying solely on Spell/Grammar-check; you will catch some things, of course, but many others, through no fault of your own, will probably slide by.

Naturally, you just want to finish, and might unknowingly speed up while proofreading and not pay close enough attention. A more in-depth explanation is that your eyes (and brain's "ears") will tend to see and hear what *you* know you mean to say. Even though you know better, in the conversation with his father, Tom's *defiantly* will quite frequently look and sound like *definitely* to you because that is what is intended to say. But to fresh set of eyes, that mix-up of *defiantly* and *definitely* will scream fowl — whoops, we meant *foul.*

Backwards, sentence by sentence.

Experts also suggest that you try reading your essay backwards — not word-by-word (how confusing would that be!?), but sentence-by-sentence. This is quite awkward, and is supposed to be. One of the reasons that proofing our own work is often inadequate is that we've become so used to reading things with sentences that (with any luck) flow well together, that we go through the motions, and our minds can wander, overlooking errors.

Think of how mindlessly we drive our vehicles; we recognize the motions and signals so automatically that — as long as things are moving smoothly — we frequently give little conscious notice of the effort we are making to drive. However, if an American were to go to London, they'd have to pay extremely close attention to all patterns and signals, or face catastrophe. Likewise — though not as lethally — by forcing ourselves to read our essays backwards, we are not lulled into a false sense of security by the smooth-flowing sound of sentences; we must pay closer attention, so any errors will be more likely to catch our eyes and ears.

Questions to Ask Yourself While Revising:

- Does the introductory sentence hook the reader and grab their attention?

- Does the introductory paragraph hold attention and give a good overview of the subject with a strong thesis statement?

- Do the next paragraphs stay focused on the main idea?

- Does every sentence lead well into the next sentence?

- Does every paragraph lead well into the next paragraph? Does each paragraph complete its purpose before moving on to the next?

- Is there a continual "flow," a smooth stream of thought that your reader will be able to follow?

- Do the last few paragraphs start leading toward the conclusion?

- Is the conclusion well-stated? Does it round out and offer closure to what the essay wants to say while complementing the introductory paragraph?

- Does the tone stay consistent throughout?

- Have you avoided over-repetition of certain phrases?

Don't forget to check the extra file we discussed in Chapter 11 for thoughts, sentences, or paragraphs you might want to include somewhere in the final product.

You might also want to ask for feedback from several sources like parents and teachers. But be careful, too much feedback can be confusing. Have one or two solid, educated critics give it a look and finish strong!

What should you do with the feedback you receive? Take all your reviewers' comments and see which ones (if any) are duplicated. If there is a particular word or phrase that all of them seem to have questioned, chances are it needs a fix. But if there is something only one of them seems to want changed, go with your instincts. Just because someone of higher knowledge sees something one way, doesn't *necessarily* mean what you said needs to be changed completely; perhaps add some minor clarification if you so choose. But bear in mind that if something seems unclear in your essay to one of your first readers, it is possible that an admissions committee will remark on the same issue.

After all of this is finished, go back over, once or twice more, using the revision bullet-points from the last couple of pages. Then put the essay away for a solid 24 hours and read it one more time before submitting it.

CHAPTER 13

You've Written It! Now WAIT! And Listen!

After you've received your constructive criticism from whomever you have asked for advice and proofreading, and all of your revision has been finished, it's time to submit that marvelous self-praising-but-humble masterpiece, and get your application packets together and prepared to be mailed.

Prep the Essay for Sending

What you want to submit to the admissions committee is not only a well-written and interesting essay, but one with a professional appearance that presents you as a student with serious college dreams.

Be sure to pay attention to the logistics and technicalities laid out for the submission process. Imagine how disappointed you would be if you spent all this time crafting an excellent application essay, but it was rejected because you didn't follow the instructions that told you how to submit it!

Formatting

You may have some direction from the college regarding the format in which the essays should be. If not, here are some pretty standard formatting rules:

- 12-pt. font size

- Times New Roman or Arial standard font

- Double-spaced with one-inch margins

- Include headers and page numbers on each page

- The title should be centered, but not displayed in bold, large, or frilly font

- Don't include pictures or clip-art

- If printing a hard copy, single-side of paper, and the paper itself should be of good solid quality and laser-printed if at all possible.

Make Copies

Before you send off your packets, make copies of *everything* that is being sent. Be sure to also hold on to any electronic files such as the one of your application essay.

You Want it to Arrive in One Piece, Right?

If you are required to submit hard-copies of your submission materials by mail, take the time and spend the additional cost to mail everything Certified/Return receipt requested. This way, you have proof of when the packet was sent (especially if the deadline is extremely close), and also of when it was received. The Post Office should be able to give you a rough idea when the materials should arrive at the destination, and if it seems to be taking too long to hear back, you can track the package to make sure it wasn't lost. If the deadline is especially close to when you are mailing your materials, perhaps try to contact the admissions office to let them know that your packet is on its way.

If the college to which you are applying is nearby, and you decide to hand-deliver your package, make sure you get a signed, dated, and time-stamped receipt from whomever receives it. Regardless of how that packet gets to the college, you want to be certain to have proof that you have done your part to apply in a timely fashion. You have worked too hard and come too far to grow careless in this all-important step of actually delivering the goods.

Waiting

Now comes that awful time that is waiting, waiting, waiting. Colleges and universities don't always respond quickly. One of our case studies heard back within days, but this is not always the case. You must be patient, go about your daily life like normal, and try to keep a positive outlook. You might not know exactly where you'll attend, but you've at least narrowed down the possibilities. It helps to remember that, come Fall, the chances are real darn good that you'll be a college student.

Under license from Shutterstock.com

You may find yourself in the position of being accepted by several institutions like many of our Case Studies were. While you're waiting for responses, you might want to start thinking along the lines of if/then, while thinking positively. *If Ohio State and Ohio University both accept me, I think I would prefer to be near a larger city, so Columbus it is . . . but if Ohio U accepts me, and not OSU, I really did like Athens, even if it's not so big.* Look at it this way: after examining all your options, every college to which you applied appealed to you for some reason or other; so regardless of which ones accept you, you have something to look forward to.

Continuing to Hone Your Writing Skills for the Future

The admissions essay is not only your key to unlocking the doorway of higher education, but also a strong reminder that you can accomplish anything you put your mind to and work hard for. Furthermore, the writing skills you've developed, either on your own or with the help of books such as this, will help you immensely. These skills will only continue to be honed even further during your college career.

. . . So, why all the fuss about writing? Why is so much importance placed on something that, according to many, has been allowed to disintegrate so badly over the past few decades?

If you think about it, the ability to read and write is the gift that separates us humans from the other living things with whom we share our world. We can marvel at the thought of those classic works having been written 500 or more years ago that can still be read today. Ancient Greek and Roman philosophers had much time on their hands to sit around musing at life, but they left us with their observations on humankind discovering itself and developing as a species. Consider, also, the importance and spiritual value placed upon the Bible, Talmud, and Qur'an.

Everything we know about human history, whether as serious as the World Wars or as recreational as professional sports, has been written down for future generations to study and understand. Any medical discoveries that will help us live longer or be more productive, are passed along and recorded through the written word. The daily newspaper, the office memo, even your text-messaging all reveal the importance and convenience of being able to communicate with each other in ways no other creature can.

We're not trying to say that you will need to be a best-selling author, but the basics of good writing are a habit that, once learned, will stay with you. Right or wrong, it can have a ripple-effect on others around you.

There are many reasons for wanting to develop good writing skills at this stage of in life, and keep them, because they will affect you more than you might have thought possible. Whether you are writing the college application essay or, in the future, business reports, the words and the way you express yourself on paper are a good indicator of your abilities and strengths as a person — and they impact others.

The college application essay is a wonderful place to start finding the writing voice throughout your life. And this does not end with your undergraduate work. If you choose to go on to graduate school, there will be more applications and essays . . . even if you find yourself one day pursuing a doctorate, you are never out of the woods, and the competition is even fiercer.

Wherever you end up in the world, know that the process you have endured and the hoops you've jumped though have brought you to this point. You've shown resilience and commitment, and the path toward college success is right in front of you. Enjoy the experience and make the most of it. Good luck out there!

SOME SCHOLARSHIP WEBSITES
(compiled June 5, 2008)

Please Note: The following websites are by no means all-inclusive; though, I have tried to generate a good sampling so you can get the idea of a few of the various types and specific areas such scholarships address. As you will find, many of the websites are only a part of a whole list formulated within that main site.

COMMON

http://www.scholarships.com/

http://www.fedmoney.org/grants/p-0-scholarships.htm

http://www.finaid.org/scholarships/

http://scholarshipamerica.org/

http://www.scholarshiphelp.org/

http://www.collegescholarships.com/

http://apps.collegeboard.com/cbsearch_ss/welcome.jsp

http://www.scholarshippoints.com/

http://www.drew.edu/depts/finaid/outsidescholarships.aspx

http://www.worldwidelearn.com/financial-aid/grants-scholarships.htm

MINORITY / RELIGIOUS

http://scholarships.fatomei.com/minorities.html

http://www.finaid.org/otheraid/minority.phtml

http://www.aicpa.org/Career/DiversityInitiatives/Pages/smas.aspx

http://www.cse.emory.edu/sciencenet/undergrad/scholarships.html

http://www.collegescholarships.org/our-scholarships/minority.htm

http://www.jackierobinson.org/apply/index.php

Christian Student Scholarships: http://www.collegescholarships.org/financial-aid/

Hispanic Scholarship Fund: https://www.hsf.net/

Jewish community Fellowship and Endowment Fund: https://jewishfed.org/how-we-help/opportunities-support/scholarships/college-scholarships

Muslim student scholarships: http://www.collegescholarships.org/scholarships/muslim-students.htm

Native American students: http://www.finaid.org/otheraid/natamind.phtml

SPECIAL GROUPS / AREAS OF INTEREST

Creative Arts: http://www.scholarships.com/art-scholarships.aspx

Humanities: http://www.finaid.org/scholarships/prestigious.phtml

Nursing: **http://www.nursingscholarship.us/**

Science & Technology: **http://www.nsf.gov/funding/pgm_summ.jsp? pims_id=5257**

Sports and Athletics: **http://www.collegesportsscholarships.com/**

Performing Arts: **http://www.donnareed.org/**

AFROTC: **https://www.afrotc.com/scholarships/types**

You will also want to check into the scholarships and grants offered within the individual institutions to which you apply. There is plenty of help out there, both from these common and internal sources. If you take some time and effort, you might be surprised to find there is plenty of financial help waiting for you.

GLOSSARY

Admissions committee: a designated group of people who review candidates to determine whether to extend admission to aspiring students

Alumnus: a graduated former student from an institution (plural: alumni)

American College Testing Program (ACT): a standardized test developed to test potential college students' abilities in English, math, reading, and science

Associate's degree: a degree granted after completion of a two-year course of study; typically from a community or technical college

Bachelor's degree: the standard undergraduate degree awarded after completion of a course of study lasting from three to seven years

Big Ten schools: a group of ten prominent Midwestern universities known for high academic standards

"College" vs. "University": both colleges and universities typically offer undergraduate, Bachelor's degree programs, but usually only universities offer graduate and professional study programs such as Master's degrees and Doctorates

College Board Standard Assessment Test (SAT): a standardized test developed to measure reading, writing, and math skills in potential college students

Collegiate: belonging or relating to a college or university, and its students

Community college: a nonresidential junior college offering courses to people living in a particular area

Core classes: a set of courses that are universally considered fundamental and basic for future coursework including math, science, English, and history

Credits: a typical Bachelor's degree requires 120 course credits for completion; each credit indicates approximately three hours of course work per week for a semester, i.e. a standard Bachelor's degree requires completion of 40 complete courses

Curriculum: the subjects comprising a course of study

Dean's List: a list of students recognized for their academic achievement each semester by the dean of the college at which they attend

Extracurricular: an activity pursued in addition to a normal course of study

Faculty: the teaching staff of a school, college, or university

Fine Arts: creative art, especially visual art, whose products are to be appreciated primarily or solely for their imaginative, aesthetic, or intellectual content

Full-ride: slang term for a scholarship that covers all costs associated with attending school, including tuition, room, board, books, etc.

GPA: Grade Point Average — the number representing the average value of the accumulated final grades throughout a course of study

Grants: money given by a certain organization, especially the government, to a student to pursue their course of study

Intramural: an activity, especially sports, which takes place solely within a school, college, or university without outside competition from other institutions

Ivy League: a group of long-established schools on the east coast with high academic standards and social prestige

Loans: money taken out by a student to pay for education expenses like tuition on the promise to repay the money at a future date with interest

Major: a student's chosen field of study upon which a majority of their studies' concentration is placed

Networking: to interact and connect with other people to establish contacts and further one's goals, especially for one's career

Personal Statement of Intent: a standard type of college admissions essay that requires the potential student to express their desire and motivation for attending that specific institution

Placement test: a test that can be administered to allow you to skip pre-requisite or required courses depending upon your level of prior knowledge of the course material

Plagiarism: the act of taking another person's work and passing it off as your own

"Public" vs. "Private": public schools largely operate on state and government funding in addition to tuition and other fees; private schools operate solely upon tuition and donations from alumni, etc. Public schools are usually far larger with more students and faculty, and less expensive than private schools

Reciprocity agreement: an agreement between the colleges and universities of two states that declares that, under certain conditions, a student from one state can attend school in the other state for the same cost as an in-state student without addition fees

Room and board: refers to the fees associated with lodging and food when attending school; can also refer to other extraneous costs such as those for certain programs, health care, and books

Scholarship: a grant of money given to support a student's education, awarded on the basis of academic or other achievement

Sororities and Fraternities: social, academic, or professional organizations at colleges and universities; "Greek" life is often Panhellenic, meaning that their status as a member extends to every known chapter of that particular group

Teacher-to-student ratio: the number of students attending an institution divided by the number of faculty teaching there; often used to indicate the standard of individualized attention a student can expect to receive

Technical/ Vocational School: typically a two-year college that mainly provides preparative courses for employment in a specific career requiring skilled labor

Thesis statement: a short statement of usually one sentence that summarizes the main point of an essay

Transcripts: an official record of a student's completed courses and the grades received for each

Tuition: the money charged for being taught at a university, college, or school

INDEX

BIBLIOGRAPHY

Bauld, Harry, *On Writing the College Application Essay,* Collins Reference, Harper-Collins Publishers, New York, 2005.

Bodine, Paul, *Great Application Essays for Business School,* McGraw-Hill, New York, 2006.

Cohen, Katherine, *Rock Hard Apps: How To Write A Killer College Application,* Hyperion Books, New York, 2003.

Curry, Boykin et al. (eds.), *Essays that Worked for College Applications,* Ballantine, New York, 2003.

Ferguson, Margaret et al. (eds.), *The Norton Anthology of Poetry,* 4th ed., W.W. Norton and Co., New York, 1970, 193, 199.

Fifty Successful Harvard Application Essays, 2d ed., St. Martin's-Griffin, New York, 2005.

Hernández, Michelle A. (1997). *A is for Admission,* Warner Books, New York.

Hernández, Michelle A. (2002). *Acing the College Application: How to Maximize Your Chances for Admission to the College of Your Choice,* Ballantine, New York.

Kramer, Stephen and M. London, *The New Rules of College Admissions*, Fireside Books, New York, 2006.

Mason, Michael. *How to Write a Winning College Application Essay, Revised 4th Edition*, Prima Publishing, Rosevale, CA, 2000.

Rankin, Estelle and B. Murphy, *Writing an Outstanding College Application Essay*, McGraw-Hill, New York, 2005.

Spencer, Kathleen, *Writing as Thinking/Thinking as Writing*, Unpublished, January 2008.

Untermeyer, Louis (ed.), *The Concise Treasury of Great Poems*, Simon and Schuster, New York, 1953, 411.

Van Buskirk, Peter, *Winning the College Admission Game*, Peterson's, Lawrenceville, NJ, 2007. Review